THE POWER
OF
EMOTIONAL COMPETENCE

A UNIVERSAL FRAMEWORK
FOR LIFE

D1738799

© JABARI JONES, MD & LOMA FLOWERS, MD

Visit Equilibrium Dynamics [EQD] at www.EQDynamics.org

Visualizations by Ken Shih

PREFACE

This comprehensive framework of Emotional Competence was developed for bright and high-achieving individuals who are action-oriented and dedicated to creating deep and lasting positive changes in their lives. Knowledge is power — and once you apply the knowledge contained in these pages you will immediately capitalize and build on your unique strengths, identify areas of growth, and become more effective and efficient in achieving your personal and professional goals. Those who apply these skills to the situations in their lives often experience rapid personal and professional growth, as adopting this framework fosters deep insight, resilience, emotional balance, and creativity in all areas of your life.

For those of you with a basic understanding of chemistry, you will recall that the Periodic Table of Elements outlines the various atoms that combine in countless ways to produce our entire physical world. No matter the time or the place, these atoms are the building blocks of everything that we see around us. The Periodic Table of Elements, therefore, is a powerful tool, as it contains universal, fundamental, and timeless knowledge about the makeup of our entire world. As a direct comparison, the Emotional Competence components outlined in this book [— the Emotional Competence Concepts, Skills, and Practices] are the fundamental building blocks of another key dimension — the emotional realm of our lives. As such, similarly to the atomic elements that make up the physical world, these Emotional Competence elements transcend time and space – they are the fundamental emotional building-blocks of our emotional lives. Therefore, this framework applies to all human beings — no matter if they were born 1,000 years ago or will be born 10,000 years from now, or if they are born in China, Nigeria or the USA — it *is* a universal framework for all human life.

This framework builds upon the thinking of many individuals throughout time. Past authors like Aristotle in his *Nicomachean Ethics* and Spinoza in his *Ethics* have described the intricate link between emotions and intellect, and have also provided guidance around how to achieve maximum satisfaction and emotional balance given the infinite number of unique circumstances we may face in life. This Emotional Competence framework is the pinnacle of this historical endeavor as it provides a universal framework to ground our knowledge and guide us in living the best life possible.

As a preview, here are three diagrams illustrating the universal Emotional Competence Concepts, Skills and Practices that underlie the framework:

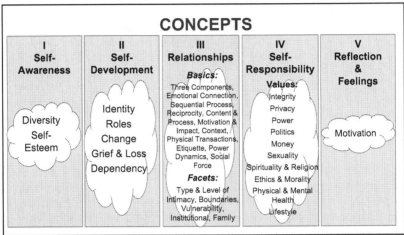

Fig P. 1 Universal Emotional Competence Concepts

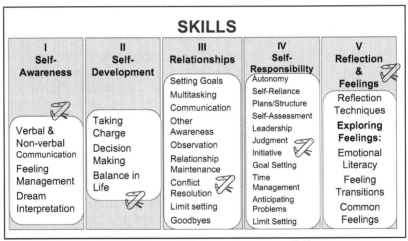

Fig P. 2 Universal Emotional Competence Skills

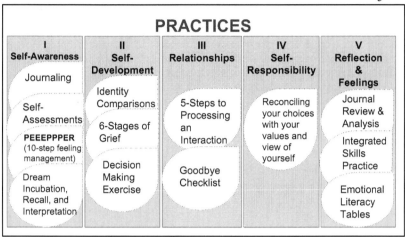

PRACTICES				
I Self-Awareness	II Self-Development	III Relationships	IV Self-Responsibility	V Reflection & Feelings
Journaling	Identity Comparisons	5-Steps to Processing an Interaction	Reconciling your choices with your values and view of yourself	Journal Review & Analysis
Self-Assessments	6-Stages of Grief			Integrated Skills Practice
PEEEPPPER (10-step feeling management)	Decision Making Exercise	Goodbye Checklist		
Dream Incubation, Recall, and Interpretation				Emotional Literacy Tables

Fig P. 3 *Universal Emotional Competence Practices*

Dr. Loma Flowers, a San Francisco-based Psychiatrist with over 40 years of teaching and clinical experience, created the first version of this framework in 1994 under the title *"Emotional Empowerment Education"*. Subsequent updates of the framework were released under the title *"Personal Empowerment Through Emotional Education and Training"* in 2003 and 2013. Dr. Jabari Jones, a Psychiatrist and Emotional Health Consultant based in New York City updated this framework in 2019 due to new perspectives gained from nearly a decade of consulting and teaching the framework.

Equilibrium Dynamics [EQD], a California nonprofit organization, adopted this framework in 2005 to teach and disseminate this approach to emotional competence nationally, including through publications. We have now worked individually and collaboratively with a wide variety of learners in lectures, seminars and workshops in the US and England[1]. These include (day and boarding) high school faculties, staff, students and parents. We lead seminars for U.S. colleges and university faculty, administrators and students, undergraduate, graduate and post graduate, e.g. premedical students[2], post baccalaureate, health care students[3], practitioners and therapists. We also consult privately on personal and professional development issues across numerous careers and at various levels of organizations.

Clients usually have identified particular issues they wish to address. Therefore, as they read the book, they can note the various sections in the big picture that relate to their issues and concerns. In related workshops and seminars, we "walk the issues" through the relevant domains and steps to demonstrate how to use the framework to analyze various situations. This analysis is the basis for selecting the concepts, skills, and practices that participants can target in their own lives for improvement. The book contains a number of protocols to practice skills. This process of analysis followed by practice on targeted skills both addresses the chosen issues and serves as a model for future applications of the concepts to new situations. This provides the groundwork for the lifelong process of achieving emotional competence. So, with deep and lasting personal growth in mind – let's start!

REFERENCES

[1] Flowers, L.K., Thomas-Squance, G. R., Brainin-Rodriguez, J.E., Yancey, A.K. (2013). Interprofessional Social and Emotional Intelligence Skills Training: Study Findings and Key Lessons. *Journal of Interprofessional Care, Early Online*, 1-3.
[2] Flowers, LK. (2005). The Missing Curriculum: Experience with Emotional Competence Education and Training for Premedical and Medical students. *Journal of the National Medical Association, 97,* 1280-1287.
[3] Thomas-Squance, G.R., Goldstone, R., Martinez, A. and Flowers, L.K. (2011). Mentoring of Students from Under-represented groups using Emotionally Competent Process and Content. *Medical Education, 45,* 1153-1154.

READING GUIDE

Each chapter outlines Emotional Competence **Concepts**, **Skills**, and **Practices** – applying these to real-life situations will help you refine and master emotional competence.

- **Concepts** are ideas that are useful to understand and consider when thinking about our emotional lives.

- **Skills** are useful in helping us to plan and direct our actions in the most constructive and effective ways possible. They differ from practices (see below) because they are less prescriptive, however, they *do* direct our actions.

- **Practices** are prescriptive processes, exercises and management techniques. Doing them consistently enhances emotional competence and maintains proficiency and sophistication in all realms of personal and professional development.

The recommended starting point for mastering the Equilibrium Dynamics [EQD] approach to emotional competence is to become as familiar with this broad framework as possible. There is a *lot* of information in here so the checklist below is included to help orient you as you read through this syllabus for the first time. This checklist is designed to help you a) recognize what you already know about emotional intelligence skills, and b) begin identifying which of the numerous topics discussed you have not yet considered. Following this guide will help you organize and integrate your current knowledge into this big picture approach. Completing this process first will be helpful when you tackle your individual issues:

1. Check mark any section in the margin that has material that feels familiar to you.

2. Exclamation Mark any topic or section that you know you find challenging, have difficulties with or you recognize as one that could help you to advance your skills.

3. Question Mark any areas that you don't understand or raise some questions in your mind.

4. After your first reading, skim through again, looking for any discernable pattern in your marks. First, note how much you already know. Next, note the challenges and questions you have identified, and which marks appear the most frequently.

5. Choose a topic that relates to a current issue in your life that you plan to address or work on first.

TABLE OF CONTENTS

A UNIVERSAL FRAMEWORK FOR LIFE
TABLE OF CONTENTS

A UNIVERSAL FRAMEWORK FOR LIFE
TABLE OF CONTENTS

INTRODUCTION TO THE FRAMEWORK

Overall this framework is designed to help learners of any age integrate and expand their emotional intelligence knowledge and skills to support productive and satisfying lives, including achieving their best performance at work or home, throughout their lives. Above all, this framework is intended to be pragmatic and to be used to deal with actual situations and challenges facing adults from all walks of life.

It is essential for your best learning that you *apply* the Emotional Competence Concepts, Skills and Practices outlined in this book. This active practice of emotional competence in your everyday life will demonstrate the powerful role that it can play. You can see your own constructive resolution of different situations and remind yourself how to avoid dysfunctional behavior by applying this framework to your life. If you have the chance to participate in a series of emotional competence workshops or seminars while you read this book they can help you apply and integrate these Emotional Competence Concepts, Skills and Practices into your repertoire. Doing this will strengthen your character, build resilience, and allow you to develop and execute more creative and constructive resolutions to challenges that arise in different areas of your life.

ADULT PERSPECTIVE

Fortunately, as adults, you have already developed some individual empowerment as demonstrated by your life experience to date. However, as we all know, although most adults get some education and training for their jobs or careers, they are rarely trained for their emotional and personal lives. Nonetheless, a great deal of our success in life depends not only upon our job and financial support of ourselves and/or family, but also upon our goals, our life management skills and our clarity about our values. This gap between training and demands often leaves us — somewhat unfairly — with individual responsibility for the major part of our own personal development.

For those of us who are older than the age of 21, most of us can recall how we felt when we turned 21. Many of us were excited to finally become legal full-fledged adults — at the same time, however, most of us were also quite intimidated by the responsibilities that adults are required to handle effectively just to eat regularly and have a stable roof over our heads. Even the commonly recommended college education provides little help towards the necessary skills for this lifelong job. Currently, there are no schools or training programs for being a "grown-up". Most of us are grateful if we were able to get some "home-training" on responsibility. Unfortunately, however, for most of us, there are gaps in our "home-training", as it did not cover a lot of the basic tasks that we face as "grown-ups". Friends, classmates, and colleagues sometimes know bits and pieces of this missing information, so pooling their knowledge with our own can sometimes help a great deal, but it is often nowhere near sufficient. Thus, we all end up learning a great deal by trial-and-error — which is a very costly and time-consuming way to learn. As one person put it, "The cost of self-tuition is high!"

There are now numerous books and articles about juggling the concurrent jobs of spouse, homemaker, and work — without adding parenting. Now that customs have shifted to allow individuals greater social freedom to elect to be homemakers and/or primary breadwinners, they often lack same-gender role models for their choices. As a result, these adults are still flying by the seat of their pants. Homemaking is fundamentally an emotional competence specialty area — as what makes an apartment or a house into a home is not expensive decorations and conventional ideas of taste; it is the warmth, comfort and nurturing to be found there, the laughter and support for tears, and the frank and respectful, safe and authentic exchange of ideas and beliefs. In order to manage all that *well* — and at the same time arrange for clean clothes and regular food, etc. — you *have* to be emotionally competent! Without these skills many people are miserable. Others may become depressed or anxious, and some self-medicate enough to lead to substance abuse.

The content of this book was developed from a combination of sources including the clinical, professional, and personal experiences of the authors. These experiences have highlighted the crucial role of emotional intelligence skills in the growth and development of children and adults. As this framework was built-out and developed over the years, new information was integrated from the constant learning that took place from the authors' lives, psychiatric practices and teaching. Because of the positive reception this pragmatic approach has received, this framework has become a central part of the Equilibrium Dynamics [EQD] approach to personal and professional development. This area of study is commonly known to psychologists and businesses as Positive Psychology or Emotional Competence, and in schools as Social-Emotional Learning.

It is crucial for adults to understand the *invisible* principles, concepts and dynamics underlying the rules and strategies we choose to use [or not use] to manage our emotions. This understanding can give us the flexibility to react constructively in every unique situation we encounter. In addition, even when we chose a less optimal course, we can plan for the higher cost and limit the damage by applying this knowledge and the related skills.

The Emotional Competence Concepts, Skills and Practices outlined in this booklet can also help adults use good judgment to make crucial decisions about applying or suspending their own rules in any circumstance. Take, for example, the rule "I never [always] lend money to close friends." On the one hand, you will know when to stick to the rules like superglue when necessary, with confidence in your own judgment. On the other hand, you will have confidence about how and when it is appropriate to make solidly grounded exceptions to your rules. One of the complexities of adulthood lies in learning how to accurately assess which situation is which. Then you have to manage your own complex feelings as you implement your best strategy in the context of your family, culture and the world in which you live.

As you read, we encourage you to learn each component of the framework as it applies to *you* first. Furthermore, we recommend you talk about ideas from this framework with friends or coworkers to maximize your learning from other adults whose knowledge will often complement your own. This can greatly enhance your effectiveness. To become really familiar with the emotional competencies needed for your personal development, we encourage you throughout your reading to apply the Concepts, Skills and Practices to current events in your life. This will give you an opportunity to coordinate both your new and established emotional competencies.

After you have applied the framework to yourself, then observe others' approaches to similar situations and compare and contrast yourself with them. It is our hope that adults who gradually develop proficiency in these extensive competencies will use them at home, on their jobs, and in every other aspect of their lives. We highly encourage you to use the competencies to deal with balancing work and play, your sexuality and safety, handling academic or work stress, surviving traumatic experiences, enjoying dating, or managing issues at home — from loneliness to marriage.

Our experience has demonstrated that success requires you to develop an extremely high degree of self-reliance and simultaneously, the skills to seek effective help the instant you need it. This intricate balance requires a complicated mix of skills. This framework is designed to both help you enhance your present emotional intelligence skills and to anticipate common pitfalls that require these skills.

It is our hope that each of you will gradually develop proficiency in every one of these extensive Emotional Competence Concepts, Skills, and Practices. Your increased proficiency will help others since emotional competence often rubs off on others and brings out the best in them. This not only supports healthy families and work environments, but also enriches your personal life and the organizations you serve in our global community. Our world needs all the help we can give it!

BIG PICTURE PERSPECTIVE

Everyone's character and personality are formed by countless events and different forces, including the genes we inherit. As a result, each person is unique and yet shares features common to all people. Similarly, although we all respond to the same basic dynamics and fundamental principles, each person develops in a unique way. In the past, the guidance of children through this process has been left to parents, schools and the church, regardless of whether or not the parents, teachers, school administrators or clergy were adequately prepared to meet this responsibility. When parents are skilled enough for the job, this might be enough, especially if children remained in the communities that had known them all their lives and were all mature by age 18.

However, unlike fingerprints which remain the same for life, our personal selves continually change from birth to death. In addition, nowadays, many of us move far from our birthplace in all kinds of ways, and frequently encounter unfamiliar forces and bewildering personalities. This further complicates a very complex, lifelong task. For better and worse, one size of personal development does not fit all, so your patterns may be very different from those of your parents, siblings and friends.

Personal change is often driven by events that are out of our control but it is frequently influenced by forces that we can tap, such as education. Consequently, to take advantage of opportunities to shape our own lives, we all need to both get into the driver's seat of any changes we can control and avoid unforced errors. Furthermore, we need to keep up with personal changes demanded by life events. The approach outlined in this framework uses the Equilibrium Dynamics [EQD] model of emotional competence development, which enlists both facts (cognition) and emotions, and teams them with good judgment *before* designing action plans.

The Equilibrium Dynamics [EQD] Program derives its name from a big picture perspective of personal development using the basic dynamics of emotional balance and the fundamental concepts and principles of emotions common to all of us and applicable anywhere and at any stage of life. Managing our own personal growth and development is a process also known as self-empowerment. This model summarizes five basic steps (I-V) necessary for anyone seeking to manage their own personal development. Within each of the five steps, various aspects are identified. These aspects hold the keys to helping you choose between constructive choices and destructive options that will cause you trouble or sabotage your goals.

The strategies included help you to recognize your own emotional dynamics and apply basic emotional principles to your everyday life behaviors and choices. These skills can enable you to weather both major and minor events more easily. In addition, they can direct your own development towards the outcomes you choose by helping you recognize whenever you reach a crossroads and guide your choice of a path. The choices we make on both large and small issues accumulate towards positive or negative results throughout each of our lives. Thus, even periodic attention to these dynamics and principles and occasional use of the strategies in this syllabus can have a significant impact on the person you are, your work, your relationships and the kind of life you lead.

OVERVIEW OF THE FRAMEWORK

Structural Divisions of Emotional Intelligence Skills

Emotional intelligence — and correspondingly emotional competence — is traditionally divided by psychologists into two **structural** areas: *intrapersonal* (inside, self) and *interpersonal* (relationships).

> ➤ <u>Intra</u>**personal emotional competence**[1,2,3,4] (Steps I, II, IV, V) includes recognizing feelings and their connection to the realities in your life, managing changes in feeling, self-discipline, decisions and planning, personal values, etc.

> ➤ The second area, <u>**inter**</u>**personal emotional competence**, (Step III: Relationships) covers the management of various types of relationships. Relationships involve communication, observations, conflict resolution, types and levels of intimacy, distinguishing motivation from impact and content from process, boundaries and limits, etc.

In reality, intrapersonal competence is on call every waking minute and whenever we deal with relationships of any kind, we blend our intrapersonal with our interpersonal emotional competence, applying the relevant skills and strategies. Extensive empirical evidence clearly indicates that acquiring and using emotional competence skills and strategies helps adults and children succeed.

Despite the familiarity and deceptive simplicity of many of the Emotional Competence Concepts, Skills and Practices addressed in this book, considerable skill is needed to smoothly and rapidly coordinate your personal needs and work responsibilities simultaneously. Managing this complicated balance well requires a constant mix of intrapersonal and interpersonal emotional intelligence skills. This framework is designed to help you improve on your present skill level. Reviewing and discussing these Emotional Competence Concepts, Skills and Practices regularly, and continuously applying them, is essential for mastery.

Functional Divisions of Emotional Intelligence Skills

In practice, emotional competence *operates simultaneously in three distinct yet overlapping dimensions*.

The **first dimension** is called the **Instant Response**. An emotionally competent instant response requires integrating feelings, thinking and good judgment *before* every action — including speech.

In this framework, *thinking, feeling, judgment* and *action* are known as "The Big Four" and their coordination underlies all emotionally competent actions. The Instant Response is a vital skill that usually combines both intrapersonal and interpersonal skills, and our expertise in this dimension depends on our development of the other two dimensions.

In practice, we are continuously called upon to respond instantly to events. This is why we need to cultivate our Instant Responses throughout the day at any moment in time. We might have to handle anything from skidding on an icy road to choosing a seat in an auditorium or responding to a personal insult or an unexpected phone call. Most of us face hundreds of these situations every week.

The following two diagrams demonstrate the instant response in the context of our entire emotional life.

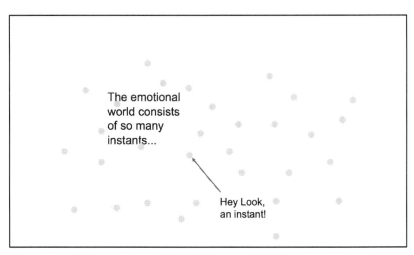

Fig. I. 1 *Each dot in the diagram represents an instant or a moment.*

The 1ˢᵗ Dimension (Instant Response):
The "here & now" integration of the "Big Four" →
Feeling, Thinking & Judgment *before* **Action**

Let's look at one!
Notice this
shaded
1st dimensional
instant...

Fig. I. 2 *The "shaded" instant goes quickly, yet involves the integration of feeling, thinking, and good judgment (ideally) resulting in action. Actions may include speech, inaction, or any other response we may have at a given moment. This is the Instant Response or 1ˢᵗ Dimension.*

The **second dimension** is the **Considered Response**. This involves the skills used to make a plan to achieve **"the best result for now and later"** and carrying out that plan. (Described in Step I: Self-Awareness, Feeling Management). The Considered Response is the intermediate dimension that uses skills necessary for making thoughtful responses to situations, taking both long and short-term consequences into account. Faust is a classic story depicting a challenge to skills in this dimension.

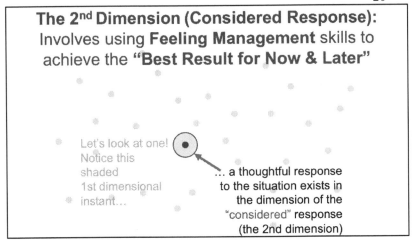

The 2nd Dimension (Considered Response): Involves using **Feeling Management** skills to achieve the **"Best Result for Now & Later"**

Let's look at one! Notice this shaded 1st dimensional instant...

... a thoughtful response to the situation exists in the dimension of the "considered" response (the 2nd dimension)

Fig. I. 3 An instant also exists in the context of a "Considered Response", which is the 2nd Dimension. This is an intermediate dimension that uses skills necessary for making thoughtful responses to a situation, taking both short and long-term consequences into consideration. It also involves the coordination of our feeling, thinking, judgment and action in a more sophisticated way to achieve the "best result for now and later".

The **third dimension** is the **Developmental Response**, our lifelong personal and professional development that both utilizes and improves our emotional competence, providing the foundation for the other two dimensions. Although personal and/or professional development can be ignored for periods of time it must be attended to periodically for lasting success and satisfaction in our lives.

Our Developmental Responses profoundly influence our identity, personality and character, and directly influence the level of emotional competence we are able to exercise. This process of lifelong development (the Third Dimension) is the backbone of this entire framework, thus, the first and second dimensions both fold into this third dimension. For easier understanding and mastery, the Developmental Response is divided into five basic steps (I-V). Understanding each of these three dimensions and their steps will help you tease out what's going on in complicated situations and begin to identify which dynamics are operating. Knowing this information helps you address each of the issues for quicker and most effective problem solving that can help you reach your goals.

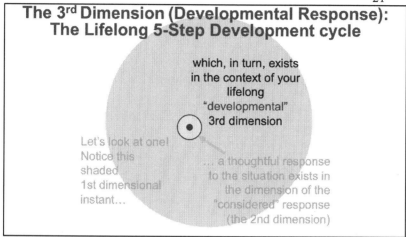

Fig. I. 4 *The instant also exists in the context of your lifelong "Developmental Response", which is the 3rd Dimension. This dimension involves our lifelong personal and professional development and includes all of our experiences and emotional competencies – it also provides the foundation for the other two dimensions. Our Developmental Responses profoundly influence our identity, personality, and character.*

THE FIVE STEPS OF THE DEVELOPMENTAL RESPONSE [3rd Dimension]

The five major *cyclical* steps (I-V) involved in the third dimension of emotional competence, the Developmental Response, are: I. Self-awareness, II. Self-development, III. Relationships, IV. Self-responsibility and V. Reflection & Feelings. These lifelong steps to emotional competence can be learned individually and the emotional intelligence skills developed in each step build on the previous step as we continually cycle through them, moving from Step V on to Step I again but at a higher skill level. Improvement in these skills can increase your self-confidence, resilience and flexibility. Many of you have probably already considered various aspects of these steps at some point in your lives.

The steps outlined in the table below provide a systematic approach to your own development and can serve as a compass to guide you through your navigation. Having it firmly fixed in your mind whenever you begin to examine a situation will allow you to use it as a checklist to analyze and troubleshoot. It will always be available after you understand and memorize it. It starts with the part that is most known to us all which is ourselves. But since we are in constant flux, the framework provides a guide to those changes.

Emotional Competence 5 Step Framework

Intrapersonal	Interpersonal
I. Self-Awareness	
II. Self-Development	
	III. Relationships
IV. Self-Responsibility	
V. Reflection and Feelings	

You will notice that the III: Relationships Step is in the middle of the intrapersonal steps. This is in contrast to the Gardner's[3,4] and Goleman's[1,2] psychological theories which structurally separate internal (intrapersonal) and external (interpersonal or relationships) emotional intelligence. However, in practice, emotional competence weaves in and out of that structure. For example, relationships are embedded in our individual lives from our conception to death, and we cannot truly develop self-responsibility without knowing how to look at others who might assume, take, share or ignore responsibilities. So, for operational and practical reasons, the relationship step fits right in the middle of intrapersonal emotional competence.

The last step of this framework, Reflection and Feelings, is both intrapersonal [you have to recognize what you are feeling and know the vocabulary to describe those feelings] and interpersonal [you have to be able to talk about feelings with other people at the appropriate level in the circumstances and to understand how to elicit the responses you need from the world that would take care of those feelings].

It might help to think of these five steps as a spiral staircase that you continually navigate, hopefully upwards. But also remember that unfortunately you can also slip down the steps under certain circumstances. That slippage is known sometimes as **regression** and it is often seen under stress, especially in children. Extra support can help get us back up. If the five steps are a spiral staircase than Feeling Fluency is the ability to walk or run up these particular steps.

The representative [not inclusive] topics or domains discussed under Steps I – V are presented in short paragraph summaries. These are designed to help you start thinking about and discussing the ideas. Exploring them in detail will enhance your skills in each section, and again, we encourage you to consider additional topics from current events in your own lives and from any psychological or self-help reading. As you read about or review the emotional dynamics and practice the emotional intelligence skills that are fundamental to your success, you can identify your strengths, assess your challenges and begin to expand your skill repertoire. Any seminar discussions that accompany working with this booklet can provide you with training opportunities and coaching while you practice. In addition, you may be able to learn from and teach your peers whose skills may complement your own. Your causal conversations and other interactions with friends and co-workers or at workshops can often provide practice opportunities. Remember, this framework was designed to organize current *and* future knowledge and skills.

Here's a brief summary of what is to follow, organized by the Developmental Response:

> ➤ **The first step, self-awareness**, begins a process of insight and related self-management skills training. This step is essential to provide the key emotions and facts about yourself necessary to coordinate any emotionally competent Considered or Developmental responses. The applications of these Concepts and development of the Skills and Practices in this step helps adults to become appropriately responsive and effective, and incidentally, allows for modelling of these competencies for others. Discussions with others can hone self-awareness and provide related self-responsibility (Step V) skills training.

> ➤ **The second step, self-development** explores the life long process of personal or professional change that accompanies every success and failure. Change can be chosen or forced on us. In either case, our Developmental Response usually accelerates in new learning situations like starting a new class or moving to an unfamiliar city. Such changes are best managed when well understood, so several keys are discussed.

> ➤ **The third step, relationships**, is the source of so much joy and pain. Simple interactions are analyzed to help you recognize some common dynamics of conversations and relationships and deal with them appropriately in a timely fashion. Using this knowledge and related skills, you can

maximize your relationship support within your family and outside of it, and minimize relationship wear and tear on yourself and your coworkers, friends and family. All together, these skills are known *as **interpersonal emotional competence*** and include the ability to start, maintain and end relationships smoothly and appropriately.

➢ **The fourth step, self-responsibility** reminds you to review the progress you have made in increasing your autonomy from childhood to adulthood and to note the gaps in the skills you have now. You can select which management skills you need to create the life you want. It includes clarifying your personal values, goals and priorities (distinct from those of your family and community), and resolving inevitable conflicts. Also addressed are integrating your values and judgment, as well as your skills in leadership, community relations and limit setting.

➢ **The fifth step is reflection & feelings.** This step outlines a journaling exercise as a model in the integration of the preceding emotional empowerment skills. Analysis of your journaled situation points the way to future applications of your skills and highlights the central role of facts and feelings — yours and other people's — in both intrapersonal and interpersonal emotional competence.

There is a large glossary of feelings at the back of this syllabus for easy reference. The feelings are separated into positive, mixed and negative emotions, with various types in separate columns. This will help you with the fundamental empowerment step of naming and talking about emotions. Whenever this skill needs further polish use these lists of common feelings. The ability to accurately identify and articulate emotions is formally known as **emotional literacy** or **feeling fluency**. As you can probably see already, it is essential for emotional competence.

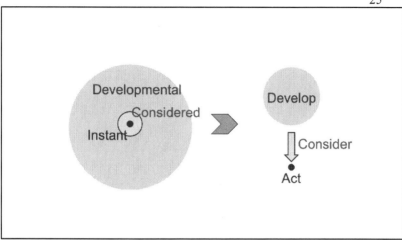

Fig. I. 5 *For the purposes of analysis and personal development (gaining and applying knowledge), we can break a moment up, and work on it using relevant Emotional Competence Concepts, Skills, and Practices that pertain to the situation being examined. By breaking down an instant into parts that we can work on, we are in fact breaking things down into their constituent emotional elements, making them easier to deal with and speak about. This makes analysis and problem solving that much more effective and efficient. In the diagram above we are transforming a contextual/dimensional visualization of what "is" (on the left) – that is, a description of contexts operating on a person in a given moment – into a "sequential and linear" diagram of "cause and effect" over time (on the right). Again, note that someone's Developmental Response abilities informs their Considered Response, which in turn informs their Instant Response – how they 'act' in any given moment.*

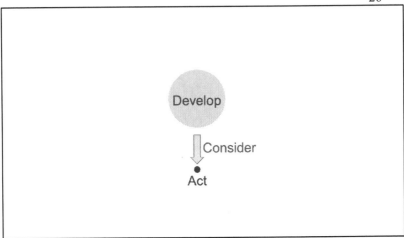

Fig. I. 6 Here is a zoomed-in view of the diagram on the right-hand-side of Fig. I.5. Working with this zoomed-in diagram we will demonstrate in the next several illustrations how Emotional Competence Concepts, Skills, and Practices combine in creating the Three Emotional Competence Dimensions — increased proficiency in these elements result in more emotionally intelligent and mature responses over time.

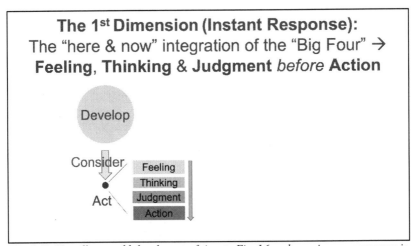

Fig. I. 7 We will now add the element of time to Fig. I.6 and examine our responses in motion. This Emotional Competence Framework breaks down the progression of the instant of action ["Act" in the above diagram] into the following sequential components – feeling, thinking, and judgment before action – again, the Instant Response.

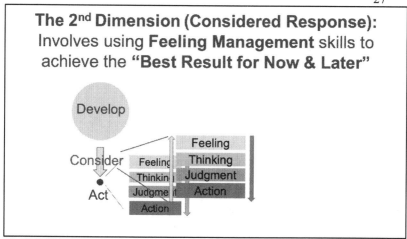

Fig. I. 8 *This sequence also holds true for the Considered Response as well – as we must coordinate our feeling, thinking, judgment and action in order to achieve the "best result for now and later". Notice how, as time progresses, responses loop and cycle in both dimensions – also notice how the 1ˢᵗ dimension folds into the 2ⁿᵈ dimension*

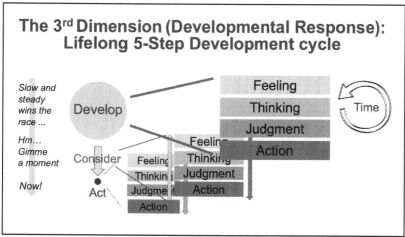

Fig. I. 9 *Over time, the same holds true for the Developmental Response – it also involves the coordination of feeling, thinking, judgment and action. Thus, the three dimensions operating in time can also be seen across categorical dimensions of feeling, thinking, judgment and action. Also, note how the 1ˢᵗ and 2ⁿᵈ Dimensions fold into the 3ʳᵈ Dimension, which is cyclical and lifelong. The remainder of this book will go into the details of each of the 5 Steps of the Developmental Response. The next several diagrams will illustrate how the 5 Steps of Development integrate into the big picture perspective of our entire emotional life.*

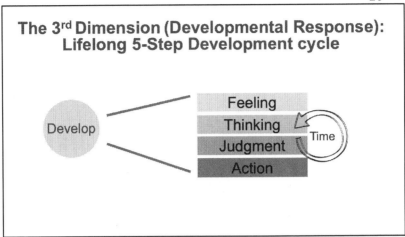

Fig. I. 10 *This figure is a "cleaned-up" version of Fig. I.9 — here we focus on the Developmental Response and how it operates over time. The Developmental Response technically encompasses the entire EQD framework since both the Instant and Considered Response is subsumed within it. Also note that "developing over our entire lifetime" is what we are "doing" with this framework.*

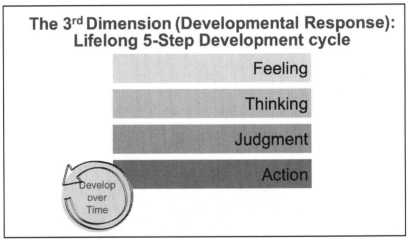

Fig. I. 11 *We have "cleaned-up" the diagram further and have now combined the arrow-circle diagram (signifying "Time") on the right in Fig. I. 10 with the "Develop" image (signifying Development) on the left in Fig. I. 10 – we are doing this to make room on the diagram for the "five steps of development", which coincide with the chapters in this book.*

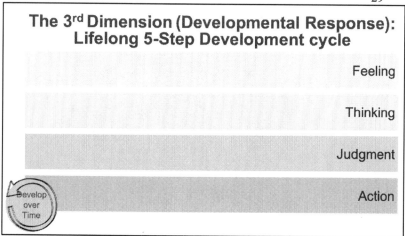

Fig. I. 12 *We continue to "clean-up" the preceding figure even further.*

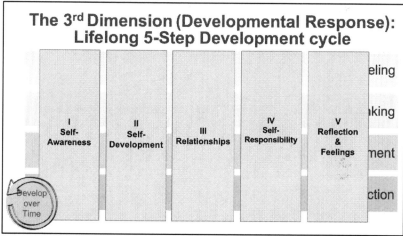

Fig. I. 13 *The goal of all the clean- up in the preceding diagrams was to add the 5-Step Development Cycle. Each step includes fundamental Emotional Competence Concepts, Skills and Practices that if applied to your life will result in personal and professional growth. The remainder of this book will go into the specific details of each of the five steps in the Developmental Response. Recall, the 1st and 2nd Dimensions "fold-into" the 3rd Dimension, thus, improvement in our Developmental Responses also improve our Considered and Instant Responses.*

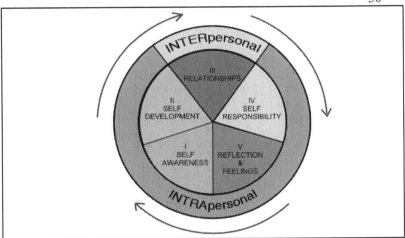

Fig. I. 14 *This diagram shows the cyclical nature of the Developmental Response – applying the framework to our lives causes us to mature and grow, and we cycle upwards. The emotional competencies (i.e., Concepts, Skills, and Practices) developed and applied in each step builds on the previous step as we continuously cycle through them, moving from Step V on to Step I again but at a higher overall skill level.*

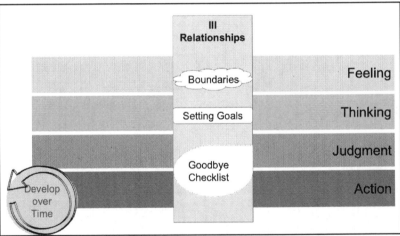

Fig. I. 15 *Review Fig. I. 13 and notice the five steps in the Developmental Response. Each step contains numerous Emotional Competence Concepts, Skills, and Practices – all of which are handled optimally through the coordination of our feelings, thinking, judgment and actions.*

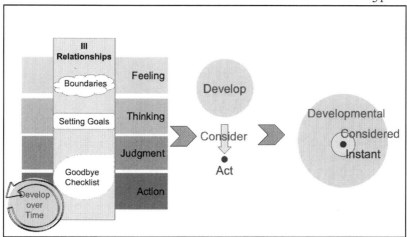

Fig. I. 16 *From a big picture perspective, no matter what situation we analyze, we can repack the Emotional Competence Concepts, Skills, and Practices back into the multidimensional moment. This diagram depicts how specific constituent components of the Developmental Response (Step III: Relationships) can be analyzed and incorporated into a constructive 1st Dimensional Instant like in Fig. I.2. [see above]. Like the Periodic Table of Elements does for the physical world, the Emotional Competence Concepts, Skills and Practices in this booklet are the building blocks of emotional life – thus it is a universal framework for life. This knowledge is infinitely powerful, as it allows us tremendous creativity to make the best possible choices for ourselves so we can live our best lives.*

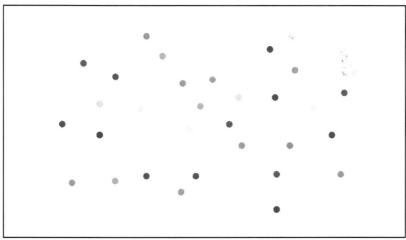

Fig. I. 17 *Each dot in the diagram represents an instant or a moment. Here's to some good moments!*

REFERENCES

[1]Daniel Goleman. (1995). *Emotional Intelligence.* New York, NY: Bantam Books.
[2]Daniel Goleman. (1998). *Working with Emotional Intelligence.* New York, NY: Bantam
   Books.
[3]Howard Gardner. (1983). *Frames of Mind: The Theory of Multiple Intelligences.* New
   York, NY: Basic Books.
[4]Howard Gardner. (1999). *Intelligence Reframes: Multiple Intelligences for the 21st
   century.* New York, NY: Basic Books.

OUTLINE & OBJECTIVES

Each chapter outlines Emotional Competence *Concepts*, *Skills,* and *Practices* – applying these to real-life situations will help you refine and master emotional competence.

- **Concepts** are ideas that are useful to understand and consider when thinking about our emotional lives.

- **Skills** are useful in helping us to plan and direct our actions in the most constructive and effective ways possible. They differ from practices (see below) because they are less prescriptive, however, they *do* direct our actions.

- **Practices** are prescriptive processes, exercises and management techniques. Doing them consistently enhances emotional competence and maintains proficiency and sophistication in all realms of personal and professional development.

STEP I: SELF-AWARENESS

Objective

Identify clearly how you feel — physically and emotionally — at various times during the week; practice talking appropriately about your feelings in a calm, clear and fluent manner with others; journal 20 minutes, 3 times a week minimum as milestones; describe a few dreams and identify your strengths and challenges in coordinating your feelings, thinking, judgment, and actions to both meet your personal and work responsibilities and achieve your goals.

Concepts

Diversity: various dimensions and paradigms, e.g. race, temperament, and personality

Self-esteem: definition, how it is developed

Skills

Verbal and Non-verbal communication: intentional, inadvertent, and their interplay

Feeling Management: coordinating feeling, thinking, judgment, and action for best results e.g. with examination anxiety, alcohol/drug use, family issues, safe sex, stress reduction, etc.

Dream Interpretation: incubation, recall and discussion of interpretation with Dream Interviewing

Practices

Journaling

Self-Assessments

10-Step Feeling Management

Dream Incubation, Recall and Interpretation

Suggested Emotional Competence goals for this chapter:

1. Describe yourself and your personality and character traits accurately.

2. Distinguish between your sense of self and other's perception of you.

3. Compare yourself to others along a continuum with respect to various characteristics.

4. Identify your feelings in a number of different, specific situations.

5. Begin the practice of talking about your feelings fluently (see Step V: Reflection and Feelings — Emotional Literacy Tables).

6. Assess your own non-verbal communication accurately.

7. Recognize the impact of non-verbal communications you transmit or receive frequently.

8. Select one practice example from your life and demonstrate how to manage your feelings, thinking, judgment and actions to meet your responsibilities and get your needs met appropriately, as you strive to achieve your goals.

9. List the basic principles of dream interviewing.

10. Complete one dream journal entry, with or without incubation.

STEP II: SELF-DEVELOPMENT

Objective

Recognize who you are, what changes you have made since becoming an adult, and what contributed to those changes. Select some future changes to control by making careful decisions about them before they occur. Prioritize your immediate major responsibilities.

Concepts

Identity: and its evolution, role definitions

Change: from loss and other causes

Loss, Grief stages: causes, management, letting go, moving on and night time dreams

Dependency Issues: dependence, independence, interdependence, codependency

Skills

Taking charge: of changes you want to make in yourself

Decision Making: the **A-B-C**'s of **Decision making** (**A**lternatives, **B**enefits and **C**osts of **D**ecisions)

Balance in your life: and emotional refueling

Practices

Identity Comparisons

6-Stages of Grief

Decision Making Exercise

Suggested Emotional Competence goals for this chapter:

1. Describe who you are today.

2. Recognize and describe some changes you have made since graduating from high school or college or choosing your first job.

3. Identify the factors that contributed to those changes from #2 above.

4. Select and describe one episode of grief that you have experienced, naming the phases and feelings you experienced, and note any you did not feel; indicate any associated actions or rituals you undertook, and relate any dream you can recall about that loss.

5. "Calculate" how to control one future change through a careful decision-making process.

6. Select three examples to illustrate differing states of dependency in your life.

7. Illustrate how you plan to balance the major demands of your life this week.

STEP III: RELATIONSHIPS

Objective

Learn how to assess your relationships with others; apply emotional competence concepts to achieve your goals for those relationships; plan how to control damage in your relationships; describe your satisfaction with your reciprocity in your relationship with your partner (if you have one); review old relationships from the perspective of your increased understanding and note any important changes in skill levels.

Introduction: accumulation of interactions, external and internal influences

Relationship Metaphor: driving a car

Concepts

Basic Facts of Relationships: three components, emotional connection, sequential process, reciprocity, content and process, motivation and impact, context, physical transactions, etiquette, power dynamics: hierarchical & collaborative, the social force

Facets of Relationships: type and level of intimacy, boundaries, vulnerability, institutional and family relationships

Skills

Relationship Skills Development: setting goals, multitasking using quick learning, communication, other awareness, observation, relationship maintenance, processing an interaction, conflict resolution, limit setting at home, school & work, good-byes

Practices

5-Steps to Processing an Interaction

Goodbye Checklist

Suggested Emotional Competence goals for this chapter:

1. Assess how conscious you are of each of the individual steps you take in any of your interpersonal interactions.

2. Assess your skills at multitasking in conversations and target one area for practice.

3. Observe your ability to learn quickly, on your feet, about other people.

4. Identify the levels of intimacy in two relationships with which you are most comfortable and in two that you find most challenging.

5. Decide your present goals for one important relationship in your life now and evaluate how well your current plan to achieve your goals within this relationship is working.

6. Predict what challenges might arise next in the relationship you selected in #5 and design a plan to control the most likely damage to occur from such an issue.

7. Critique your current conflict resolution skills.

8. Assess your separation skills (managing goodbyes) and review your dependency issues in this context.

STEP IV: SELF-RESPONSIBILITY

Objective

To articulate and discuss your attitudes and feelings towards self-responsibility; observe when and where you practice it or avoid it and how — intentionally and unintentionally; design a couple of plans to facilitate one or two specific changes you would like to see in yourself.

Concepts

Values and Judgments: integrity; privacy vs. openness vs. secrecy, attitudes and feelings; power; politics; money; sexuality; spirituality & religion — internal experience, external signs, observances etc.; morality & ethics, definitions, traditional, contemporary and individual practice; physical and mental health — prevention, sleep, safety, maintenance, e.g. exercise, diet, stress reduction, and health care treatment or choices

Life Style: authenticity and image

Skills

Autonomy: the paradox of freedom; discipline

Self-Reliance: dynamics of self-care and seeking help; initiative

Plans and Structure: End Result Desired (ERD), goal setting, developing plans to meet challenges; time management, priorities, "back planning;" anticipating problems

Self-Assessment: analysis and explanations without blame or excuses

Leadership: attitudes and feelings towards community responsibility; limit setting

Judgment: good and bad

Practice

Reconciling your choices with your values and view of yourself

Suggested Emotional Competence goals for this chapter:

1. State one end result you desire in your journal then name the goals you need to reach to achieve that end result; distinguish between long and short term goals.

2. Design a realistic plan to achieve at least one or two goals during this year.

3. Assess your self-discipline and plan how to achieve and maintain the level you require to reach your goals.

4. Identify 3 of your leadership roles to date; note any common themes.

5. Discuss one example where it was difficult for you to use good judgment.

6. Estimate your level of initiative in comparison with your peers in school and work.

7. Discuss the current process of self-assessment that you use to evaluate your performance and estimate your tendencies for self-blame, excuses, self-praise and realistic apportionment of responsibility.

8. Explain how you are dealing with your own judgments of others at work/school.

9. Compare your sense of integrity and need for privacy with others you know.

STEP V: REFLECTION AND FEELINGS

Objective

To summarize what you have learned about your emotional competence from this framework and devise a plan to integrate your new knowledge into your life; to clearly identify your feelings and expand your vocabulary of feelings.

Concept

Motivation: feelings are the driving force in our lives

Skills

Reflection techniques: meditation, prayer, music, exercise, yoga, water, etc.

Exploring Feelings: emotional literacy, feeling transitions, common feelings (monitoring your tolerance, role of psychotherapy)

Practices

Journal Review and Analysis: to support regular entries and to integrate your emotional competence education, using reflections, self-evaluation and goal setting

Integrated Skills Practice: recounting, recording, diagramming, analyzing, identifying skills needed to resolve (e.g., feeling management, decision making, limit setting, plans, etc.)

Using Emotional Literacy Tables: to facilitate clear identification of various emotions as well as increase your comfort and familiarity with appropriately including your major feelings when discussing and/or writing down events

Suggested Emotional Competence goals for this chapter:

1. Summarize verbally any changes you can detect in rereading all your journal entries from when you began reading this book to the end.

2. Analyze one particular problem situation in your life using the "Integrated Skills Practice" outline.

3. For the identified problem in #2 integrate the Emotional Competence Concepts, Skills, and Practices covered in this framework to devise a plan for personal change – consider *all* components that may be required to enact the change, for example: a) identity development, b) goal setting, c) planning, d) effective coping, e) problem-solving, f) rewarding-relationship development, and g) increased personal gratification, etc.

4. Implement the plan you developed in #3 and record your results.

5. Use the Emotional Literacy Tables (a list of common feelings arranged by type) to:

   a. Facilitate clear identification of various emotions.

   b. Encourage yourself to make subtle differentiations between feelings.

   c. Increase the feeling vocabulary used in your journal.

   d. Enhance your verbal fluency and accuracy about feelings.

FIRST FUNDAMENTAL PRINCIPLE

The first principle in this approach is:

> **Emotional competence is a practice.**

This means that emotional competence is not just knowledge but actually applied knowledge that directs actions. It is the capacity to access your emotional knowledge and filter it through your thinking and judgment to construct the most effective actions you can think of to take care of your needs and feelings throughout your life.

The unusual aspect of the EQD approach to developing emotional competence skills is the comprehensive framework underlying this approach. The seemingly simple framework is unique in its broad base and the fundamentals of its structure. These are both essential to a versatile practice of emotional competence, one that allows for unlimited modifications with changing circumstances. As a result, it is important to master the basic concepts and principles early and practice continually to achieve proficiency.

The practice of emotional competence would be difficult enough if all you had to consider were yourself. However, it is always essential to keep in mind two other complicating factors. First, life is an accumulative process, which requires constant adjustments. Second, your life involves all kinds of variables over which you have little control such as other people, the systems people have developed over centuries like laws and customs, and the physical world. Although we can know only a tiny part of these vast areas of knowledge, in order to reach our goals, big or small, we have to navigate the events we encounter. Emotional competence is the key to this navigation.

STEP 1

SELF-AWARENESS

DIVERSITY

SELF-ESTEEM

VERBAL and NON-VERBAL COMMUNICATION

FEELING MANAGEMENT

DREAMS and NIGHTMARES

SELF-AWARENESS

INTRODUCTION

This section focuses on essential strategies to increase your **self-awareness.** Self-awareness is the keystone of all sophisticated life management and the first of the five steps of personal development. Self-awareness is often called **insight** and is defined as the ability to observe your inner self and your actions objectively, as you move through your day. You can watch yourself in the moment or think about it afterwards. It is important, at this point, to distinguish self-awareness from the more problematic traits of self-consciousness, self-absorption, self-centeredness, and self-interest; although they can, of course, coexist with insight.

Many serious difficulties in life arise first as minor issues that can easily be addressed before they escalate. But this requires at least one of the people involved to have the **insight** to see the issue and to fix the problem. Therefore, self-awareness is an essential part of a satisfying home and work life that most of us would prefer. Fortunately, self-awareness is a skill that can be learned with conscious practice, and utilized whenever helpful.

Everyone also has to figure out how they learn best — including learning emotional competence — and address those needs too in some reasonable way. Unfortunately, everyone has to develop some tolerance to frustration as they learn new things as well as some self-reliance [Step V] until gradually we become able to structure our own learning, e.g. as you are doing by reading this.

PRACTICE: JOURNALING

We recommend that you **begin journaling regularly** this week to facilitate and reinforce your learning and to strengthen your self-awareness and other emotional competence skills. If you do not already have a journal, buy any kind of notebook that you can write in. Get in the habit of recording what you are doing and how you feel about it for **at least 20 minutes, three times a week**. Just the process of such writing helps people process feelings. Research has shown it can positively promote general health. In the long run, it can also probably save you time by helping you identify problems and solutions more quickly.

Even if you hate to write, we urge you to jot down (or type) a few notes about what you are thinking about and your feelings about it, three times a week. There is a mental process that only seems to occur with writing about an issue that has important differences from what occurs when thinking or talking about it. Journaling will activate that process. Review your journal from time to time, at least once a month, and use these overviews to see how you are doing. There is nothing like periodic journal reviews for maintaining self-awareness and documenting your personal growth. It also helps you to recognize when you are stuck and need help.

CONCEPTS

I) DIVERSITY

Diversity means **differences**, any kind of difference. In the latter part of the twentieth century in the USA, diversity became frequently associated with race, ethnicity, culture, religion, gender and sexual orientation, etc. because of the anti-discrimination laws. The big picture of diversity extends far beyond these few categories and self-awareness requires you to be familiar with where you fit into the larger world with respect to any number of variables.

Think about your own personality. Which adjectives would you use to describe yourself accurately — rather than either modestly or a "rose-colored" view? What are the common adjectives others use to describe how they see you? Do you agree with them? This section of the framework will give you an opportunity to begin to see yourself clearly from the inside, and reconcile it with how others see you from the outside.

Look at the following examples of personality traits, arranged in paradigms. Some are opposites; others represent the intensity of a single characteristic from missing to dominant. Compare yourself, your colleagues and others you've seen or heard about. On which paradigms are you in the majority, which in the minority, which at an extreme? When do certain trait show themselves, and where not? Think about how you have changed over time and your behavior in different situations. What feelings come to mind? Which traits do you find regrettable and which likable?

Increasing levels of cultural and other diversities across the US require all of us to be able to handle differences smoothly to preserve peace in all our communities. This is a true test of emotional competence. Understanding yourself in the context of diversity will probably enhance your ability to achieve this level of expertise, by increasing your awareness of differences and their infinite varieties.

II) SELF-ESTEEM

Self-esteem is defined as the level of confidence in our own worth or abilities – it is also known as self-respect. Having a healthy self-esteem means having a positive and *accurate* self-image, with healthy levels of self-love, vitality, creativity, and assertiveness. It also means being able to tolerate the vulnerability that comes with being in relationships and resilience in the face of disappointments. For us to develop a healthy level of self-esteem it is important for us to have had the experience of being empathized with, validated and protected (— *but not over-protected)* by caretakers growing up and peers. Some individuals with low self-esteem manage their intense feelings of vulnerability and low self-worth by lashing out at others, or by building an inflated and highly unrealistic sense of themselves – both may have the unintended impact of "putting people off". Another possible consequence of having an inaccurate view of ourselves is that we may set unrealistic goals – this may result in a deep level of dissatisfaction and impair our capacity for sustaining effort.   Look at your life right now — do you have relationships where you feel known, admired and supported? Why or why not? How can you start building them? If you need help doing so or have issues functioning due to low self-esteem we would suggest you seek help from a mental health professional.

PRACTICE: SELF-ASSESSMENT DIVERSITY PARADIGMS

Listed below are some examples of personal characteristics. They are arranged in paradigms to stimulate discussion. Consider your own personal characteristics compared to others in your life with respect to any number of human variations on a scale of 1 to 10. Feel free to list your own paradigms in your journal.

Temperament, Personality, Appearance, Talents and Style
[Score from 1-10]

one extreme	midrange	other extreme
1…….2………3	4…..5…..6…….7	8…..9…..10
quiet	responsive	talkative/garrulous
self absorbed	considerate	self sacrificing
shy	assertive	aggressive
insecure	confident	arrogant
delicate/sensitive	adaptive	tough/unchanging
submissive	conforming/ conventional	defiant/rebellious
pragmatic/ unromantic	sensible	idealistic/dreamy
competitive	alternating/both	collaborative
optimistic	realistic	pessimistic
disinterested	interested	motivated /enthusiastic
follower	independent	leader
calm/rational	excitable/quick tempered	irrational
unfocused/messy	focused	focused/organized/ tidy
outgoing/friendly	responsive	isolated/aloof
participant	watcher/observer	loner

charming/polished	basic good manners	gauche/socially inept/rude
local/accented speech	standard speech	multilingual
happy/cheerful	pleasant/even tempered	moody/irritable/ critical
tall	medium height	short
athletic	mobile	uncoordinated/ restricted
unattractive	plain/ordinary	attractive/striking
heavy	normal weight	thin
stiff/awkward	relaxed	sensual/graceful
slow mover	average speed	quick
stylish/fashionable	appropriate dress	dowdy/unkempt
contextual learner	learning is usually easy	analytical/detail oriented
methodical approach	observant	intuitive
brilliant/flashy	average intelligence	plodding/pedantic

Values
[From 1-10 ~ What is *your* score?]

one extreme	midrange	other extreme
1.......2.........3	4.....5.....6.......7	8.....9.....10
financially ambitious	financially satisfied	philanthropic
upper social class	middle class	lower social class
pleased with social class	satisfied socially	embarrassed by current social position
religion is a private matter	Indifferent to any religious practices	proselytizing [of my religion or disbelief]
I am entitled to what I can take/get, fair or not	I like gifts and am entitled to them whether or not I reciprocate	I earn what I get; gifts make me uncomfortable
cheating/stealing is always OK	If someone gives me too much change, I keep it	cheating/stealing is never OK
lies & lying are an everyday part of my life	social lies only, usually	always choose truth
private/reserved	public speaker, public kisser	exhibitionist/ I put risqué photos on social media
I love gossip and like to stir up trouble	I enjoy gossip, if it is not too unkind	I always try to calm people down, a peacemaker
monogamy	an occasional affair is OK	open marriage/relationship

spendthrift	budget follower	saver
financially dependent on others/government	self-supporting	independently wealthy
I focus on caring only for myself	I occasionally help others who ask for my help	I have a strong sense of duty to care for and help others (family and/or community members)
I arbitrarily back-out of promises/obligations that I have made with others	I sometimes fail to keep obligations when other pressing matters arise	I always carry out my duties and obligations

SKILLS

I) *VERBAL AND NON-VERBAL COMMUNICATION*

It is extremely important to be aware of how you communicate because, as you may already realize, your communication style impacts *every* interaction you have with others. It can even impact those who overhear it, hear about it, or see it. Many people are not *fully* aware of their usual communication patterns that others, including children, see or hear during *every* contact. Listen to yourself, and observe yourself as you relate to others at home, at work, and along your commute. Don't forget phone calls, text messages, emails and social media postings in this regard. Begin to assess what you generally like in your communications and note anything you wish to change about your style — or dislike in others. Check to see if you practice any of the qualities you dislike — and consider changing your style.

Since most of us begin our adult lives as unmarried singles, we need a wide range of communication skills for developing new relationships. The skills we have as we enter adulthood will have been learned from our family and school contacts. As a result, when we move into other communities and various jobs most of us need to further develop our skills to meet new situations. These improvements can help you build and keep the relationships you want – and a lack of skills can get in your way. [More about communication in Step III: Relationships]

VERBAL COMMUNICATION

Verbal communication is the mainstay of relationships. Hence, you need effective skills in this area to convey your ideas and feelings clearly. Without this capacity, you will be constantly misunderstood, and possibly misjudged as far less knowledgeable and capable than you really are. This can be a serious problem, e.g. when dealing with businesses, supervisors, strangers or school personnel.

We recommend that everyone practice describing feelings with accuracy, fluency and appropriateness, and extend their vocabulary to achieve **emotional literacy**. (See Step V: Reflection and Feelings.) This skill will allow you to avoid being silenced by complicated or strong emotions, and it will also help you express your messages effectively and constructively, even in public situations. Such articulate expression also models for children and peers how to avoid the dilemma between silence and profanity, which is far too prevalent in contemporary American speech and rarely contributes to a positive resolution of transactions.

Effective communication through speech requires **clarity of ideas**, a deliberate choice of **words**, clear **pronunciation** regardless of accent, and appropriate **intonation** — all of which can vary from region to region. Statements are often most effective when they begin with clear **"I" messages**. (More on this later in Step III: Relationships.) Of course, written communication has to convey everything you wish to be understood in the words and phrases chosen, which together generate a tone. Since each person differs from others with regard to their skills, begin your self-awareness by assessing how easy others find it to understand you in casual conversation compared to your peers. How often are you asked to repeat yourself? What feedback do you get from your friends or your family?

For the listener and responder, oral communication requires **attentive listening** to the nuances and details as well as the general gist of what is being said, because people often do not express themselves precisely or accurately, especially when agitated or tackling complex ideas. Moreover, if you travel at all, you will encounter more and more people from different backgrounds with varying speech patterns and verbal proficiency. As a result, conversations are often aided by **reflective listening**, thinking about what you just heard before you respond. How would you compare yourself to others as a speaker and as a listener?

Clear communication makes it easier for everyone, e.g. families, friends and children to understand exactly what you want, especially if you want them to do something, or to cooperate or negotiate appropriately. Finally, we recommend that you learn to convey your ideas and feelings clearly, accurately, rapidly, and succinctly when dealing with others on your job, whether they are supervisors, coworkers or supervisees.

It is helpful for everyone, for both personal and work success, to learn a fairly standard version of American speech. This means that you or your friends may then have more than one language, dialect or speech style in their repertoire and that *your* preferred speech may differ at times from those around you. It can be helpful to explore your feelings about this.

NONVERBAL COMMUNICATION

Nonverbal communication passes between people all the time, and it can be inadvertent/unintentional or deliberate/intentional. It is generated by one person while having an *impact* on others – often times outside of conscious awareness. When we observe someone doing or saying something, cells in our brains called **mirror neurons** automatically mimic their movements – thus we automatically replicate their experience in our own minds.   Research also has shown that when we interact with others, parts of our brain automatically "read" their emotions, this phenomenon is called **emotional contagion**. These phenomena make up an automatic non-verbal channel of communication that we continuously have with others.   Those of you who have pets will be very familiar with deliberately using nonverbal communication with them too. Gestures such as waving, shrugs, giving someone the finger, smiles and scowls are easily recognized and understood within our US culture. Unintentional non-verbal communication occurs inadvertently, i.e. you had no idea you were "saying" anything and/or it may be an unavoidable consequence of something you *are* doing, but for another reason.

There are both positive and negative aspects to non-verbal communication. The advantages are in its silence, and its capacity to sometimes convey a great deal of information remarkably succinctly. Non-verbal communication is also independent of language, so we tend to use it in countries whose language is foreign to us, and when we can't hear or speak for some reason. It is also used to temporize because of its indefinite nature. Sign language was developed for hearing impaired families and is a sophisticated form of nonverbal communication. It is now also used by many hearing families with toddlers before they can talk.

The limitations of nonverbal communication are mainly in its lack of specificity. Misunderstandings can easily arise from this ambiguity and the consequences of such miscommunications are varied. There are cultural conventions in non-verbal communication, as well as in verbal, and miscommunications may arise from the same gesture meaning different things to different groups.

A good example of non-verbal communication is **clothing**, which generates feelings and judgments in everyone — whether or not it's theirs — such as wearing a suit or a miniskirt. In choosing clothing, some of the important issues and feelings involved are: personal preference, institutional convention, appropriateness to the weather or the occasion, current fashions, and impact on others.

It is often helpful to consider **manners** as one kind of non-verbal communication. The use of **good manners** and *the omission of their use*, **bad manners** or neglect, sends very powerful messages to everyone within sight, hearing or smell. Be sure you know what constitutes good and bad manners at the institutions in your life. There are always a number of established traditions in any organization and it is important to learn what they are soon after you arrive so that you can decide how to handle them.

Vocalizations that are not words, but recognizable sounds, exist in every culture and are also powerful communications. These include grunts, shrieks, laughter and sighs, etc. In addition, the tones, inflections and innuendoes of words can communicate as much or more than the words themselves. This may be deliberate or unintentional; nevertheless, you need to become aware of your own habits and range in this area too. Unconscious sighing, for example, can convey boredom or exasperation to anyone within hearing, who is likely to feel insulted, disrespected or unsupported. You may unintentionally lose important opportunities if you make such noises unconsciously.

II) FEELING MANAGEMENT

There are a number of basic steps involved in managing **the link between feelings and behavior** with consistent maturity, which requires continual self-regulation. Skillful management of these steps is essential for personal empowerment and success in your work and relationships. The absence of skills in feeling management often results in poor self-control, which in turn can derail you through, e.g. procrastination, interpersonal conflicts, addictions, eating disorders or unwanted pregnancy, to list a few.

You can gradually learn the steps of feeling management, and then slowly gain mastery by doing them a few times every day. Poor skills are much better than none. If you persist, the steps become familiar, and then faster, and finally automatic and rapid. Of course, many people lapse, particularly when first learning. However, keep in mind the goal of mastering the steps, and use them to both prevent missteps and also to *remedy* situations — from trivial to crucial — that you feel you have mishandled.

THE MAJOR FEELING MANAGEMENT STEPS: THE CONSIDERED RESPONSE

Introduction

Whenever an **event** happens in your life, you respond in some way. For example, you lose something extremely important, or your partner wants to talk first thing in the morning, or your child throws a tantrum. Hundreds of such events happen every day, and each time, you respond instantly, often without pause or thought. It may be an action — which includes speech — like frantically searching or walking away, or it may be a deliberate "non-action" such as pretending you did not hear or silently ignoring the other person.

This **Instant Response** is the **1st dimension** of emotional competence and for it to be constructive and effective it requires a balance of *thinking, feeling,* and *judgment* **before** action, "The Big Four." It is easiest to learn how to make effective Instant Responses through learning the slower **Considered Response,** then speeding that up until you can do it off the cuff, in an instant.

When you *consciously* decide whether or not to do something, you are *making a choice*, and then you can also choose *how* to act.

This process can greatly empower you and it is named the **Considered Response.** It is the **2ⁿᵈ dimension** of emotional competence. Fortunately for us, many events are routine and totally problem-free so you often have enough time to consider your responses. There are a number of skills involved in this process. Once you learn the basics, it is important to practice well and often so that your ability to respond constructively *in the moment* will improve in parallel.

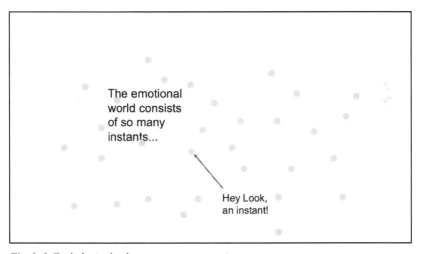

Fig. 1. 1 Each dot in the diagram represents an instant or a moment.

The 1st Dimension (Instant Response):
The "here & now" integration of the "Big Four" →
Feeling, Thinking & Judgment *before* **Action**

Let's look at one!
Notice this
shaded
1st dimensional
instant...

Fig. 1. 2 The "shaded" instant goes quickly, yet involves the integration of feeling, thinking, and good judgment (ideally) resulting in action. Actions may include speech, inaction, or any other response we may have at a given moment. This is the Instant Response or 1st Dimension.

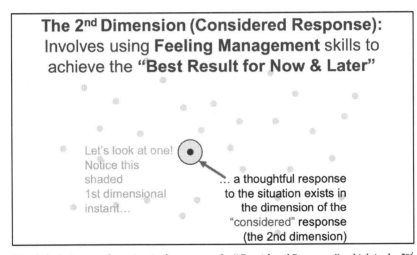

The 2nd Dimension (Considered Response):
Involves using **Feeling Management** skills to
achieve the **"Best Result for Now & Later"**

Let's look at one!
Notice this
shaded
1st dimensional
instant...

... a thoughtful response
to the situation exists in
the dimension of the
"considered" response
(the 2nd dimension)

Fig. 1. 3 An instant also exists in the context of a "Considered Response", which is the 2nd Dimension. This is an intermediate dimension that uses skills necessary for making thoughtful responses to a situation, taking both short and long-term consequences into consideration. It also involves the coordination of our feeling, thinking, judgment and action in a more sophisticated way to achieve the "best result for now and later".

Overview

Let's take a detailed look at the tricky parts of our response process, which occur when the situation is complicated or strong emotions become involved. Such occurrences require the use of reason or **thinking** including **judgment** to mediate between **feelings** and **action**s, i.e. feeling management. This ten-step basic **Feeling Management Process** assists you in **analyzing the facts of the event, understanding your feelings**, and then **strategizing** to devise a **plan** to **direct** your own **behavior**. Lastly, it reminds you to filter these possibilities, using good judgment (Step V: Self-Responsibility — good & bad Judgment) to select the optimal plan to achieve **the best result for now and later.**

The crux of these ten steps is **"The Best Plan for Now and Later"**, which is why that phrase is often used by our trainees to describe this process. Although it is often easy to do something that seems fine in the moment, it is much harder to devise an action that serves both the moment and the foreseeable future. Identify a couple of problems you could have avoided—personally or as a family or community—if only you had considered both *long* and *short* term consequences.

It is important to note that only two steps in feeling management require action: steps one and eight. You take no action during the other eight steps* — these steps require clear thinking, using reason and judgment. Also, it is often useful to discuss these thinking steps with a friend or mentor as you go through them. This discussion will also aid in the development of feeling fluency as you incorporate your feelings appropriately into your conversations about situations.

This Considered Response skill will serve you well everywhere. It is this careful **integration** of feeling, thought, judgment and action that is essential for your **empowerment** to accomplish your goals as an adult and create smoothly functioning relationships that help you thrive. As you may know, repetitive or extremely disturbing events may require the help of a professional counselor or therapist. If you are wondering about it, don't hesitate to check it out with someone.

Whenever you find yourself in the middle of a situation, look at what you are doing. Locate where you are in the ten-step process of feeling management, and be sure you have completed all the previous steps before you move through the rest. If your plan does not work the first time, go back to step one. Take a TIME OUT, and rethink the whole situation. Follow the second plan. Repeat this until you are satisfied with your results or you have "tried everything reasonable," that you can think of, and must accept the situation as it is. As you begin to practice these steps, consider how often you actually behave this way now, and watch as you gradually increase your use of this technique, and your skill with it. Check to see what differences it makes in your life.

We have been told by a number of people that ten steps are hard to remember, especially at first when you need to use them the most! We agree! However, when a task — like getting dressed in the morning — takes ten steps or more, it is important not to skip any. Otherwise, it will not be done completely. **So, here's a memory aid:**

Either **Pepper,** or as the kids preferred, **"PEEEPPPER!"**

P	Steps 1 & 2	= **PA**use for **Pause & Analyze**
EEE	Steps 3, 4 & 5	= three **Emotion** steps
PPP	Steps 6, 7 & 8	= three **Planning** steps
ER	Step 9 & 10	= **Evaluate** & accept **Results**

PRACTICE: FEELING MANAGEMENT 10 STEPS

(*No overt action in these steps*)

1. **TIME OUT**, i.e. when an event happens, pause while you do the following steps, # 2-5. This seems simple but many problems come from impulsive responses that do not allow for any thinking or reflection about consequences.

2. * **ANALYZE** what happened i.e. recount what happened, include the *whole* story, and arrange the sequence in **chronological order**. Recount it like a movie. This will help you understand clearly what happened, and help **distinguish cause and effect**. It often helps to write it out, double-spaced with wide margins. If you word-process it, you will find the reorganization of the facts much quicker. Include your **feelings**, adding ones that occurred to you after the event in the right margin. Remove any information not directly related to the story.

3. ***NAME ALL YOUR FEELINGS** as precisely as you can, and use Part VI to help you include all the feelings you experienced throughout the event. If you censor or omit feelings, your subsequent plans and actions are more likely to be flawed.

4. ***SORT YOUR FEELINGS** into **relevant, anachronistic** and **irrelevant** categories. Relevant feelings are directly related to the event. Anachronistic feelings are past and future feelings evoked by the event because: it is similar to a previous experience often years old now, or, e.g. it evokes frightening possibilities. Irrelevant feelings are associated with other concurrent events that have nothing to do with the specific event being managed.

5. **FACE *ALL* YOUR FEELINGS**. This means process them by exploring and examining them. It is not necessary to wallow in them, or to whip them up into more than they are, nor blame somebody else for them. They are yours. Treat them carefully, like a carbonated beverage. Allow yourself to experience all the feelings, and tolerate or endure them *without acting on them*. They will often gradually dissipate or convert while you "watch" yourself go through this process. Processing feelings in this way is often facilitated by crying, journaling and talking.

6.   ***CHOOSE THE BEST RESULT for NOW and LATER.** Use good judgment and careful consideration of your desires and the likely consequences. Discuss if there's time.

7.   ***PLAN HOW** to make that "best result" happen. Think carefully and be realistic. Talk it over with others if you can. Break it into steps, if necessary. Identify any help needed: quality, timing, quantity, source and method needed to obtain it. Set timelines.

8.   **FOLLOW YOUR PLAN** and *nothing but* your plan, but do *follow* your plan. Act.

9.   ***EVALUATE YOUR RESULTS**: examine what worked, what didn't and why.

10.   ***ACCEPT THE RESULTS and MOVE ON**. This is easiest when you are at least partially successful, but it is always necessary at some point. Poor outcomes may require you to go back to the beginning and manage your feelings about disappointment.

III) DREAM INTERPRETATION

Dreams, including nightmares, are an excellent source of "inside information" about yourself. Everyone has 4-5 dreams a night whether or not they remember them. Many of you may remember having had dreams that were helpful to you, or nightmares that frightened you. You are probably also familiar with common dream themes, such as flying, being chased, taking an examination or falling.

Dream interpretation fits into a very broad context of **work on dreams** which includes:
- Physiology of Sleep and Dreaming
- Dream Recall Research in sleep lab and clinical practice
- Manifest Content of dreams: analysis, description, categorizing and manipulation
- Latent Content of dreams: **interpretation**, application of meaning and manipulation, i.e. incubation or pre-sleep suggestion
- Dream Art: representational, dream inspired and therapeutic

Traditional Theoretically Based Organization of dream analysis:
- Various cultural traditions of dream interpretation
- Freud (1856-1939)
- Jung (1875-1961)
- Medard Boss (1903-1990) (Phenomenological)
- Fritz Perls (1893-1970) (Gestalt)

Delaney's Process Based Organization of dream interpretation methods[1]:
- Cultural Formula Method [includes amplification] (Bible, Egyptian, Jung, Artemidorus)
- Psychotheoretical-Formula Method (Freud, Jung)
- Associative Method [Includes Symbol substitution] (Freud, Jung, Cartwright, Bonime, Krippner, Fiss, King, Craig)
- The Emotion-Focusing Method (Fritz Perls)
- The Personal Projection Method [Intuitive](Ullman and Zimmerman)
- The Phenomenological Method (Boss, Delaney, Craig, Flowers)

Dream interpretation, using the phenomenological method, **Dream Interviewing,** is a very important recent development in the world of dreams. It is conceptually simple but like many skills, it is not easy to become an expert. It takes a great deal of practice to become proficient, like mastering Emotional Intelligence Skills. However, also similarly, it is a technique that can give you important and useful information about yourself, even as a beginner. If you discuss dreams with your close friends, using some of the steps of dream interviewing, you may be surprised by how much insight you gain from even a partially understood dream.

Remember that **all interpretations are hypotheses**, and application of the insight should be thought through carefully, not followed blindly. Use the feeling management steps. Those of you who learn the technique fairly well will be able to get an accurate enough impression of the meaning of your dreams — and possibly those of others — and may find them extraordinarily useful in everyday life. We will only have time for a brief introduction here in this book, but those of you who are particularly interested can pursue further reading. You can work on your own, with another "dreamer" you trust, or in workshops or private consultations.

Next, we will take a look at how to remember your dreams (dream recall) and how to start a dream journal.

PRACTICE: DREAM INCUBATION and DREAM RECALL

Dream incubation, otherwise known as pre-sleep suggestion, means directing your dreams to work on a problem for you while you sleep. It is easily combined with the dream recall routine.

Dream incubation is a 5-step process:

1. Provide yourself with a dream journal, such as a binder or spiral notebook, or use your journal.

2. Day Note: Just before you go to sleep, write the date and the title, "Day Note." Then, write a brief paragraph about the major events and feelings of your day.

3. Incubation Question: Next, write the title "Incubation Question" and underneath, write a little about the issue that is on your mind. End with the specific question or issue you would like your dream to answer or clarify. Do not ask for magic. Be as precise as you can about your wording. Ask only what you would really like to know, e.g. How can I motivate myself to study more? Why am I having trouble doing as well as I'd like?

I need a dream to help me study more effectively. Then repeat the question to yourself as you fall asleep.

4. Recall Preparation: Leave the dream journal, pen, and a light by the bedside within easy reach.

5. Dream Recall and Recording: Upon awakening, immediately think back into the night, and write down any dream, dream fragment, thought, or feeling. Always write something. Then give each dream a title for easy reference. Be sure to distinguish waking ideas from dream ideas. No drugs or alcohol the night before and awaking to quiet, rather than an alarm clock, facilitates recall.

PRACTICE: DREAM INTERPRETATION USING THE DREAM INTERVIEW METHOD

THE DREAMER'S PREPARATION STEPS FOR DREAM INTERVIEWING:

The following dreamer's preparation steps can expedite both the interpretive process and the resulting insight, when completed prior to the actual dream interview **by the dreamer**:

1. Dream incubation (pre-sleep instruction)
2. Dream recall
3. Dream recording
4. Dream diagramming
5. Dream outlining

THE BASIC STEPS OF THE DREAM INTERVIEW

The interviewer's role is in italics.

1. **Description:** This is the dreamer's descriptive definition of the major dream images.
*The interviewer asks questions to help the dreamer make a good description. (See Step II: Self-Development – **Identity Comparison Practice** for questions to ask in order to elicit descriptive definition for each dream image)*

2. **Recapitulation/ Restatement:** *The interviewer tells the dreamer what they heard about each image the dreamer describes.* The dreamer helps the interviewer get it right.

3. **Bridge:** This is the interpretation itself. Where does the dreamer recognize the descriptions in waking life as a part of themselves, or as a part of someone/something else? Remember, consider the dream as a **metaphor**. Where in life does the dreamer have similar feelings in a parallel series of events*? Ask questions, don't suggest.*
The interviewer helps the dreamer recognize what it stands for in their life.

4. **Testing the Bridge:** The dreamer checks out that everything else fits between the dream and the match with waking life.
The interviewer checks out that the matches make sense.

5. **Summary:** The dreamer explains what they think the dream means and how they figured it out.

SUMMARY

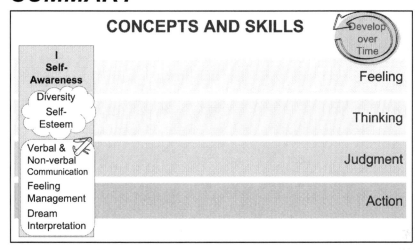

Fig. 1. 4 *Step I: Self-Awareness Concepts and Skills*

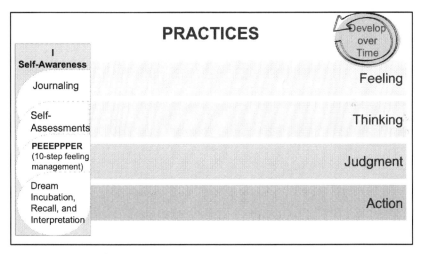

Fig. 1. 5 *Step I: Self-Awareness Practices*

REFERENCE

[1]Delaney, Gayle. (1998). *All About Dreams*. San Francisco, CA: Harper Collins.

SUGGESTED READING

Delaney, Gayle. (1993). *New Directions in Dream Interpretation.* Albany, NY: SUNY
    Press

Equilibrium Dynamics [EQD]. (n.d.). Retrieved from
    http://www.eqdynamics.org

Flowers, L.K. (1998). The Changing role of 'Using' Dreams in Addiction Recovery.
    Journal of Substance Abuse Treatment, 15, 193-200.

Flowers, L.K. (1996). The Dream Interview Method in Addiction Recovery: A Treatment
    Guide. *Journal of Substance Abuse Treatment, 13,* 99-105.

Flowers, L.K. (1995). The Use of Presleep Instructions and Dreams in Psychosomatic
    Disorders. *Psychotherapy and Psychosomatics, 64,* 173-177.

Gayle Delaney PhD. (n.d.). Retrieved from
    http://www.gdelaney.com

Kramer, M and Glucksman, M. (2015). *Dream Research.* New York, NY: Routledge.

STEP II

SELF-DEVELOPMENT

IDENTITY

CHANGE

**LOSS, GRIEF, LETTING GO,
and MOVING ON**

DEPENDENCY ISSUES   **TAKING CHARGE**

DECISION MAKING

BALANCE IN YOUR LIFE

SELF- DEVELOPMENT

INTRODUCTION

All individuals grow and develop *involuntarily* throughout their lives, physically and otherwise, gradually aging and maturing. Each of us can also elect to *voluntarily* participate in that process. **Self-development** is the conscious, guided process of inner change we go through in life when we choose to grow personally and emotionally to accommodate our own goals, achievements and experiences.

A conscious focus on your own self-development will help you to keep pace with the demands of your life. Without this deliberate effort to develop as a person, you increase the risk of sabotaging your ability to achieve your goals. Each goal you set or achieve will require its own set of changes, from losses as well as gains. As you may already have experienced, your emotional responses to the *impact* of such events and your management of those emotions can enhance or hamper your future growth.

Two major factors that precipitate change in individuals are **life events** and **decisions,** including **indecision**. They can enhance your self-development or damage it. Thus, the more you know about managing both life events and decisions, the more capable you are of positively influencing and directing all those aspects within your control. We discussed making thoughtful responses to life events under the ten-steps of Feeling Management, the Considered Response. This section is about techniques for making decisions that control life events, and managing the subsequent changes for continuous constructive self-development.

As you may already have experienced, when people are overwhelmed by their lives, it impacts everyone in their circle. As a result, if we care about our friends and family, each of us has a responsibility to "carry our own weight" as much as we can by managing our lives to the best of our abilities. Self-Development is essential to keep up with those management challenges in success or setbacks.

CONCEPTS

I) IDENTITY

Who you are and how you think of yourself is called your **identity.** It is always important to know yourself in order to make appropriate choices for your situation. This in turn will affect your achievements. However, once you do know yourself, you will find that your identity evolves and changes continuously throughout your life, sometimes very rapidly. You must expect considerable **identity evolution** as a young adult if you are to mature appropriately. Similarly, older people can also expect identity changes with aging. It is important to monitor your own identity because changes in a person's identity are also often fluid. They can change back and forth at various times, even day to day! Dreams often help you with awareness of changes in your identity. Keep an eye on your dreams to see what you can learn about yourselves as you navigate these numerous changes.

Throughout life, some adults change a lot and others much less. Listen carefully to what others *tell* you about how they see you. These remarks may be spontaneous or said in response to your own self-descriptions or questions: "How do I look?" Listening to what others say about themselves and others will provide you with perspective on their opinions of you, and you can evaluate their feedback in this context. You will learn about yourself and **your image** in the process, even if others' impressions are not consistent with your view of yourself/identity. When your views differ from the views of others, always consider how *you* might be giving a misleading impression of yourself. This will give you an opportunity to modify your behavior should you choose to do so. Friends can often help each other reconcile their image with their sense of themselves by using kind, tactful, honest and clear feedback. Finally, consider an adult you know with a mismatch between their sense of self, your perception of that adult, or their **public personalities**. What feelings does that mismatch evoke in you?

II) *ROLE DEFINITIONS*

Everyone has a variety of roles that they fulfill professionally and personally, such as being a son or daughter and church deacon, a parent and a dentist, a spouse and a paralegal, a committee chair, a musician, or a coach and a waiter, etc. Since wearing a number of hats at the same time can be very taxing, look at what you are expecting of yourself at this time in your life, as you name and count the roles you have committed to fulfill.

Now, examine your feelings about your various roles. These feelings are often grounded in *how* you came to assume this role. Was it a first choice or through random circumstances? Are you feeling lucky, for example, or are you disappointed, or both? Notice how these circumstances influence your feelings about your role now. Also, think about what kind of role models your teachers and family were for you, remembering that you can learn a great deal from both good and bad examples. How do you wish to be different or the same?

PRACTICE: IDENTITY COMPARISON

Please follow this outline description (below) of yourself and **write in your journal,** for comparison in a few years.

MY IDENTITY:

Name: _____

Date:_____

Please print for easy reading.

Physical description of myself (include race/ ethnicity, size, hair, clothes today etc.)

My major life goals now are:

My personality: (Include at least 5 adjectives) + any unique aspect of myself (state "generic" if not unique in *any* way)

My most striking feature is:

My essence, or core characteristic: (One essential quality, without which you would be someone different)

Relevant association: (a brief anecdote about becoming an adult that illustrates your identity)

Positive feelings and judgments about myself:

Negative feelings and judgments about myself:

III) CHANGE

Change is fundamental to life and is both the cause and the result of growth and development. Consequently, change is inevitably accompanied by both losses and gains. Since change is known as one of the highest causes of **stress**, it needs skillful emotional management to be beneficial and empowering, and not destructive.

Think about what you were like as a child and what you went through because of the *impact* of the changes that made you an adult. Also, what changes do you see in yourself since you became an adult? In addition, the events of your adult life can influence you, and that causes certain changes too. Identify a couple of such changes that come to mind now. Think what rituals you used to manage the impact of gains, such as a promotion or marriage, or a lovely new home. Explore the emotions you experienced from negative events or changes such as having an accident, having [or not having] a baby or being fired, etc.

Change can also be an exciting opportunity to redesign your life. As your life evolves, you will have many occasions to do this to accommodate your changing needs. Perhaps you will marry or travel or have a family, adjust to an empty nest or accommodate stepchildren, retirement or widowhood. How do these changes feel like a gain, or a loss, or both? What appeals to you about redesigning your life? What do you find daunting? Consider what other roles you could assume in this new phase. Think about how you managed your feelings and actions through a previous transition and what you can learn from that experience.

IV) LOSS, GRIEF, LETTING GO and MOVING ON

LOSS

Fires, death, divorce, job loss or decrease in social status because of loss of wealth are all losses that affect us emotionally. That pain is especially great when the loss is permanent. Among the most devastating of these losses is the death of a parent, or child. Similarly, losing a beloved pet can also cause significant grief. There are innumerable more **commonplace losses** too, such as losing an earring or a wallet, getting a dent in your new car, your wedding gift not arriving on time for your friend's wedding, or missing a party because your partner is sick. Each loss produces some version of grief.

People often say, "Forget about it!" or "Oh, I just get mad," or "I don't get mad, I just get even," or "No big deal, I'll just get another one". We suspect many people do so to avoid feeling the pain of grief *because they do not know how to manage it*. But this framework will help them navigate those feelings so that they can at least explore them privately, at some point. Otherwise they will stockpile the pain and risk it overflowing in a flood someday.

There are now a wide variety of books available and websites on the Internet offering help to anyone with grief and loss.

GRIEF

Grieving or mourning occurs when we have a loss and have to let go of important relationships, roles, things, etc. Psychiatry generally recognizes five stages or phases that can, of course, overlap. This framework adds a sixth.

> Phase 1: Numbness and **disbelief** (shock)
> Phase 2: **Yearning** for missing the person (can include **bargaining** and guilt)
> Phase 3: **Protest** (angry, irritable)
> Phase 4: **Despair** (grieving, sad, bereft, desperate, hopeless)
> Phase 5: **Detachment** and moving on (ready to let go, newly relinquished, hopeful, reintegrating your life without the lost person etc.)

> [Phase 6] **Anniversary reactions** are a common enough phenomenon that we add them as a phase as well.

The feelings of each stage move through us like the waves of a tide coming in, and eventually receding.

Adults often feel the need to restrain grief publicly or in front of others. Nonetheless, it is crucial for them to not permanently stifle grief, but to grieve each loss, privately at least, no matter how silly it may seem or upsetting it may be, or how tired you get of crying about it, or how **vulnerable or unmanly** crying makes you feel. It is actually an error to believe "there's no point in getting upset because there is nothing I can do about it anyway." What you *can* do is grieve. This promotes emotional healing, which in turn supports physical health. Both of these are crucial to healthy adults. Time only heals if *you* allow the healing in that time. Watch for these feelings of grief and grieve completely each time. This really means to just let it run its course. It will happen by itself if you get out of its way. When you fail to **grieve**, you stock pile the unfinished grief in an "emotional closet", and sooner or later the door won't close properly. That's when emotions are likely to come spilling out all over your life at very inopportune times.

When we **mourn the future**, we experience feelings of grief, sadness and loss in regards to wishes, hopes and dreams that will not materialize due to a permanent loss. This frequently occurs with the loss or disability of a loved-one. For example, a young child is diagnosed with a terminal illness and the parents not only grieve for the eventual loss of the child, but also for all of the hoped-for special occasions and life-events that were expected for the child – such as graduations, marriage, and children of their own. Another example is when an athlete has a severe career-ending injury – when these occur the athlete's mourning includes the loss of a hoped-for successful sports career. There are many circumstances where we mourn for the future. Can you think of any instances where you have mourned the future?

Unfinished grief is a major source of the **anachronistic feelings** mentioned under Feeling Management (Step I: Self-Awareness – Feeling Management). Unfinished grief also contributes to many depressions. Anger may leak out indirectly or physically, e.g. in high blood pressure, or inappropriately too, perhaps, as crankiness or bad temper. Overt expression of feelings of grief often make other people uncomfortable, so they sometimes discourage grieving, frequently seeking to distract, or "cheer up" a person who is appropriately grieving. You can reassure them you are fine and keep grieving when and where appropriate.

Change from positive events can be just as emotionally wrenching, but the negative feelings are often counterbalanced or even eclipsed by the pleasure in the change. Think about what you were like before a helpful change in your life. Then, think what you went through emotionally and practically because of that event and note the differences in yourself afterwards. What other good experiences have you had that made you change? What happened to the associated feelings of loss?

Many losses, such as not getting a class you were ambivalent about or losing touch with a difficult parent, can produce very mixed and conflicting feelings, none predominating. Unfortunately, these events are often harder to grieve than those losses that are more straightforward, clearly positive or negative.

Anticipatory grief is a way to pace your grieving when a loss is inevitable. It helps to minimize the chances that you will be overwhelmed and not able to function when the final moment comes. For example, if you have a friend or relative who you know is dying, or someone has been accepted to college in another state you can begin the process of grieving while you can still enjoy their company. This early grieving makes the final break much easier to manage when the person is actually gone. (More on Goodbyes in Step III: Relationships.)

There are a number of **social rituals** we use to manage the impact of changes, whether welcomed or deeply lamented. Think of the rituals you have participated in. e.g. funerals, graduations, showers and confirmations. Are there ones you have avoided? Were you trying to avoid dealing with the feelings they evoke? Think of what helps you to tolerate the feelings of loss. Different cultures have various traditions for assisting with change and loss such as blues music, an extremely effective, cultural model for processing grief.

LETTING GO

Many of the changes that impact you will involve others in your life, e.g. parents divorcing or remarrying, and moving out of the home you knew, friends who drop out of school or continue when you drop out. These events can evoke a combination of positive and negative feelings in you also, some of which are surprisingly strong. When this happens to you, use your feeling management steps to resolve your feelings and decide whether or not to keep in touch, and how, etc.

Remember, it is important to privately acknowledge whatever feelings you experience and not prejudge them. Then you have to process them through thinking, speaking and/or crying and writing, and eventually come to terms with them, without acting out (or "acting up," "showing out," "blowing up" or "losing it," etc..,. — you can tell by the number of phrases how common this is!). **Verbal eloquence** is as powerful a tool as histrionics or violence when it is well used. One of your tasks for empowerment is to become verbally eloquent about these issues rather than physically demonstrating your feelings. **Repressing** your feelings, or pretending to yourself and others that they are not there, is often very destructive in the long run, too.

Repression is quite distinct from the necessary skill of **containing** your feelings until an appropriate time and an appropriate place to express them. You can use containment to **compose yourself** after tears. It is easiest to practice containment with minor losses – this practice is a good rehearsal for managing more serious losses.

Nighttime dreams frequently deal with losses in your life, sometimes anticipating the inevitable ones. Your dreams will often point out problems to you that you don't consciously see, and guide you in a more productive management direction. If you do remember a dream of loss, write it down in your dream journal to what you can understand about the dream's message.

MOVING ON

When you move on, and accept a loss, it can bring a pleasant feeling of liberation. You can also hold onto parts of the old relationship that you value or have incorporated into yourself, or your life, at the same time as you relinquish the lost person or home, etc.

Find your journal — or start a new one — and write a paragraph about one loss that you have recently experienced. Note the feelings and any changes it caused, where you are in the phases of grief, and how you plan to move on. Be prepared to talk to someone about this experience of journaling.

PRACTICE: 6-STAGES OF GRIEF

The 6-Stages of Grief:

Phase 1: Numbness and **disbelief** (shock)
Phase 2: **Yearning** for missing the person (can include **bargaining and guilt**)
Phase 3: **Protest** (angry, irritable)
Phase 4: **Despair** (grieving, sad, bereft, desperate, hopeless)
Phase 5: **Detachment** and moving on (ready to let go, newly relinquished, hopeful, reintegrating your life without the lost person etc.)

Phase 6: **Anniversary reactions** are similar feelings that come back a year later, or at special times that remind you of the original loss you grieved.

The feelings of each stage move through us rather like the waves of a tide coming in, and eventually receding. You can be in several stages of grief concurrently and at different intensities. It is crucial to manage your feelings in detail about each loss that you encounter. Use feeling management at each stage to fully process your feelings around grief and loss.

The following are some questions that will help you through the process of emotional healing after a loss – use your journal to write your responses:

1) Is there anything that you wish you had said to them or did for them?
2) Is there anything that you wish they had said to you or did for you?
3) What good and bad experiences have you shared with them?
4) What unfinished business do you have with them?
5) What impact has the person had on you?
6) What changes in yourself have you undergone from knowing them?
7) What will you take with you and treasure?

V) DEPENDENCY ISSUES

Another major dimension of change for adults relates to dependency issues. You may have first experienced this aspect of change when you left home as a young adult or were employed for the first time. This is a change towards more **independence**, though it can also be accompanied by increased **dependence**, e.g. needing to be taught how to cope. As seniors or disabled adults, we often feel the change towards more dependency.

Some of you may also be aware of your concurrent **interdependence.** By interdependency we mean that you need people to help you at times, without leaning on them totally, and at the same time you help others occasionally too. This is a kind of **balanced** dependency. Your peers, coworkers or siblings and family members are usually excellent resources and sources of support in this regard.

For success, it is important to be able to shift fluidly between all three states of dependency, depending upon the needs of the situation. Problems usually arise when you are locked too firmly into one mode or another – especially if you are not aware of it. This can make you unable to accommodate new circumstances easily. Sometimes you need to shift many times in a single day, and then not for a week.

Now, think about where you are on this major identity continuum, from **dependent to independent**. Identify some ways in which you are **dependent,** ways in which you are **independent**, and ways in which you are **interdependent**. How flexible are you, on a 1-10 scale, with 1 being quite stuck and 10 very fluid?

Did you change with regard to dependency (either at home, work or school) after you made a recent decision? Are you still in transition?

As a future reference point, write four paragraphs in your journal that you would be willing to read aloud on the following questions:

1. How you assess your overall dependency today on all three dimensions?
2. Where you would like to be more independent?
3. Where you would like to be more dependent, i.e. more taken care of, less self–reliant?

4. Where you would like to be more interdependent? How is it useful?

CODEDEPENDENT RELATIONSHIPS

Codependent relationships are a type of dysfunctional relationship where one person supports or enables another person's immaturity, addiction, irresponsibility, or under-achievement. Often, a codependent individual finds themselves repeatedly playing the role of the rescuer, caretaker or confidante and fear that they will be abandoned or rejected if they set limits on their ability to provide support. Codependent individuals often have an excessive reliance on others for approval and self-worth – they may also unconsciously satisfy their need to feel competent and esteemed by comparing themselves to the dysfunctional relationship partner. These relationships can develop between spouses, friends, children, siblings, clients, and co-workers and often involve a "neglect" of our own needs and an obsessive need to "control" another person's behavior. It is important to examine your current relationships and determine if you are involved in any codependent relationships — if you are, the Part III: Relationships section of this manual can help you manage the transition to a healthier relationship.

There are also now a wide variety of websites and books available that offer help to anyone who is in a codependent relationship — if you find that you are overwhelmed by these relationships and need additional support we suggest you seek help from a mental health professional.

SKILLS

I) TAKING CHARGE OF YOUR LIFE

As mentioned earlier, changes in a person's identity occur over time and are often fluid. Therefore, it is important to be **aware** of your own identity and its changes so that you can **take charge** and make some **decisions** about the changes you **want** to see in yourself. This empowers you to become more like the kind of person you wish to be. You are too important to leave to chance!

Taking charge of any changes you want to make in yourself, and making the necessary **decisions** about them is an essential part of being effective. For example, you are more likely to be successful as an adult if you decide what kind of work you wish to do to support yourself; or how you will spend your time to just keep your mind active and your life purposeful if you do not need to or are unable to work. Similarly, your relationships will be more satisfying if you decide what kinds of relationship you want — friends, movie buddies, lovers, caretakers, admirers — and which people fit that role best. Choosing housing requires parallel decisions, and indecision or passivity can lead to you finding yourself in a situation you hate. Any choice to not decide or to just go with whatever force is pushing you at the time is in fact a decision.

II) DECISION MAKING

The decisions you make direct your life in one direction or another. It is therefore very important to make decisions carefully, recognizing what they mean, for now (**short term**) and later (**long term**) as well as to **assess the impact** they will have on your identity, the balance in your life, and the achievement of your goals. Sometimes a small decision can have a large impact, so **all decisions are important**.

As you mature and your identity evolves, if all goes well you will see yourself facing more and more choices. You will face more and more decisions about what you are going to do from moment to moment about hundreds of small things, and sometimes a frightening number of large issues.

On the following two pages is a simple, basic model for decision-making: The **A-B-C**'s of **D**ecisions! **A** = Alternatives, **B** = Benefits, **C** = Costs/Consequences. This simple exercise will help you identify your strengths and weaknesses in making decisions. Select a small decision that you are currently in the process of making. Follow the instruction sheet and answer the questions as directed *in your journal or a separate notebook.* Stay self-aware and notice your changing feelings as you go through the steps.

It is usually very helpful to discuss your experience after you have finished.

PRACTICE: DECISION MAKING EXERCISE

Instructions

Sound decision-making is an extremely valuable skill to have, and you may already be skilled. Nonetheless, you can use this exercise to double check your process and highlight the **feelings** you experience. Please answer the following questions that guide you through the **A-B-C's of D**ecisions!

I.   Write all the answers to the questions below in your journal, following the model of the worksheet on the next page.

II.   List all your feelings about each entry on the facing/opposite page of your journal.

1. What is the **D**ecision you have to make?

2. What **a**lternatives do you have? I.e. what are **all** the choices you **could** make? It is **rarely** just either/or, so **look** for those 3rd and 4th **A**lternatives. Be creative. Write them in opposite 1a, 2a, 3a, and 4a on the worksheet.

3. What **B**enefits are there for each choice? Write in opposite 1b, 2b, 3b, and 4b.

4. What negative **C**onsequence/**C**ost is there for each choice? Write in opposite 1c, 2c, 3c, and 4c.

5. Grade each **B**enefit on a 1-10 scale: 10 = fantastic/ideal, 1 = barely worth anything.
 Write in the score at the end of each **B**.

6. Grade each negative **c**onsequence on a 1-10 scale. 1 = almost nothing bad/a very minor **C**ost to you, 10 = terrible. Write in the score at the end of each **C**.

7. Note the **B**enefit score and subtract the **C**ost score. Write the answer in the margin by each **A**lternative (1a, 2a, etc.) and circle it.

8. Your best **A**lternative is probably the highest score. What is your best choice? Circle and * your best **A**lternative.

9. What do you now think of your **A**lternatives that have a negative score?

10. What are you actually going to do? Why? What **C**onsequences can you anticipate now, and how are you going to handle them?

Write in your journal using the following Worksheet format:

I have to decide the following:

_____
_____
_____

Alternatives, Benefits and Costs: (a, b, c)
1a._____

_____
1b._____
_____**Score**_____
1c._____
_____**Score**_____
2a._____

_____
2b._____
_____**Score**_____
2c._____
_____**Score**_____
3a._____

_____
3b._____
_____**Score**_____
3c._____
_____**Score**_____
4a._____

_____
4b._____
_____**Score**_____
4c._____
_____**Score**_____

III) BALANCE IN LIFE

Since your life involves a combination of activities, you are constantly called upon to select which ones you will engage in at any one moment. Some are for fun, some are responsibilities you choose, some are requests by others to reciprocate help you have received, and some are selected to help achieve your goals and so forth.

In addition, whenever your life requires a great deal of time and effort, this in turn can reduce personal and family time significantly. This is especially true for ambitious adults who choose to devote most of their time to school or work. Limited time and energy require that we choose how much of each we do. It is important to balance your choices in a way that makes you the most effective in all of the activities you do, especially where there are time sensitive milestones to reach.

Emotional "Refueling" or "recharging" is very important when you are feeling down, or just drained from all your activities and responsibilities. Think about which activities or relationships make you feel better, that restore your energy and/or soothe you, e.g. music, meditation, exercise, sleeping, hugs, walking and talking on the beach. It is important to know what they are, how each one helps to restore your energy and perspective, and then remember to use them whenever you find the need. You have to budget energy a bit like money, balancing the income with the spending to not run out and overdraw your emotional accounts.

Time management is a combination of decision making and balancing your life. Take a look at your current commitments, and assess the balance. What time have you allocated for health maintenance — physical, spiritual and emotional — including adequate sleep? How much for journaling? Is this the correct balance for you at present? (See also Part IV: Self-Responsibility). And lastly, does it add up to 24 hours or less?

SUMMARY

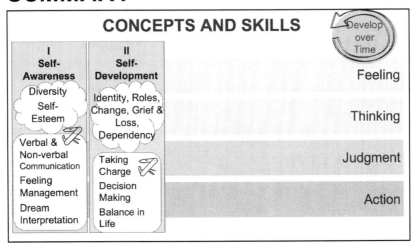

Fig. 2. 1 *Addition of Step II: Self-Development Concepts and Skills.*

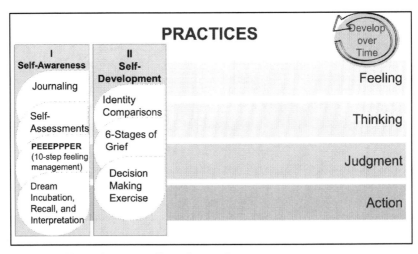

Fig. 2. 2 *Addition of Step II: Self-Development Practices.*

STEP III

RELATIONSHIPS

RELATIONSHIP MANAGEMENT

INTERPERSONAL TRANSACTIONS

**BASICS of
RELATIONSHIPS**   **FACETS of
RELATIONSHIPS**

RELATIONSHIP SKILLS

GOODBYES

RELATIONSHIPS

INTRODUCTION

Millions of books have been written about relationships over centuries in countless languages. And this is just one indication of how important they are to people. Can you name a couple of other indications? Professionally, relationships are fundamental to all the service professions such as health care, law, and education.

Everyone is usually very content when a relationship is going well and not inclined to examine it too closely. The questions come when tensions arise. Although most difficulties in relationships arise from the relationship itself, many are caused by external events, such as transitions in life. For example, you may have changed homes, cities, jobs, lovers or marital status. Most of you have already negotiated many such situations in your life and dealt with the changes in relationships that result. In the self-awareness and self-development sections, you began to look at yourself and how that knowledge will help you to recognize your part in both the difficulties and successes inherent in your relationships. In this section you can further assess and develop your current knowledge of some basic facts and facets of relationships as well as your skills of communicating, reciprocity and awareness of others, etc.

This section will also give you an opportunity to explore some of your newer relationships to decide early on how to manage them. You can also reevaluate the changes that have occurred in old relationships. As you learn more about your relationships, you will increase your understanding of both the processes underlying them and of the automatic everyday interactions you have without thinking about them. We will start with some basic concepts and fundamental dynamics that you can build on for the rest of your life. You can also adapt what you learn about one relationship to other relationships you have.

The outline that follows has proven helpful for keeping relationships in good working order and running smoothly as well as for troubleshooting when problems arise. How many of you have a problem with a relationship now? How many truly satisfying relationships do you have now?

RELATIONSHIP METAPHOR

Self-awareness and sensitivity to others is necessary to do well in relationships. Many factors go into learning how to manage relationships skillfully. Driving a car is a useful metaphor for managing relationships. How many of you can drive now? Let's look at the parallels between managing relationships and driving a car.

First, you have to manage yourself as a driver, which is like managing your personal needs and feelings: get in the correct seat, adjust the seat so that you can see, set all the mirrors so you can see in front and behind, music volume off or adjusted so that you can easily hear sounds around you, etc. Decide on taking passengers, and whether or not you will use a cell phone — even with an earpiece — while driving, knowing that more accidents occur when you do.

Second, you have to manage the car, which is like managing your body, your speech and your actions: key in the ignition, brake on or off, lights, wipers, steering etc. This also includes maintenance, such as oil, air in tires and gas.

Third, you have to know the rules of the road, the traffic laws. This is like knowing social etiquette and the rules, policies and procedures of the organization or institution you are involved with. Just like speed limits can change from place to place and safe speeds vary with weather conditions, social rules also change with changing contexts, e.g. from person to person, place to place and time to time.

Fourth, you have to be aware of the other cars on the road, which may or may not be well driven. Drive safely to avoid accidents, regardless of whether or not you are "in the right." This is like being sensitive to other people, so there are no "crashes" or even "fender-benders."

Fifth, you have to know where you are going or you will drive around wasting gas and wearing out your car and tires for no purpose, unless your goal is just the immediate pleasure of the ride. However, in the latter case, you cannot be surprised that you don't get somewhere specific.

Consider how much time you have in any interaction to think about each factor. What do you have to do to get extra time to think? Is there a parallel here with feeling management? (See Step I: Self-Awareness).

CONCEPTS

I) BASICS OF RELATIONSHIPS

a) THREE COMPONENTS

The simplest relationships have three parts: **you, the other person** and **the interactions** that happen **between you**. We are all familiar with how the complexity rises exponentially from this basic unit when there is an increase in the number of people involved, e.g. a family of three, a work team or a reading group. Each person has to manage multiples of the same three components, plus groups seem to take on lives of their own that have to be dealt with too.

b) EMOTIONAL CONNECTION

> ➤ Lasting relationships require reciprocal effort (avoid one-way streets)

All relationships involve an emotional connection of some kind between two or more people. It is now well known how important it is for caregivers to bond with their babies and vice versa in order for the baby to grow and thrive. This infant bonding also requires a physical connection and there is evidence that skin-to-skin connection is an important part of this bonding. Your own bond to your parents or whomever took care of you as a child is your model for your emotional connections. These emotional connections— found in all relationships — are the driving force for relationships. If the connection is weak or tenuous — as is often the case with coworkers — the demands of the work will easily supersede the relationship. If the emotional connection is strong with a coworker, there is a risk of it superseding the job. Hence the military rules limiting "fraternization."

As mentioned previously in Step I: Self-Awareness (the Non-verbal Communication section), research has shown that when we interact with others, parts of our brain automatically "read" their emotions. This phenomenon, called *emotional contagion,* happens mostly outside of our conscious awareness. Therefore, it is not only what we say, but also our real emotional tone at the time of an interaction that has an impact on those around us. Likewise, the feelings inside those who are around us during an interaction have an impact on us as well – oftentimes without us being aware of it. Also, when we observe someone doing or saying something, cells in our brains (called *mirror neurons*) automatically mimic their movements – thus we replicate their experience in our own minds. These phenomena are the building blocks of empathy and attunement with others, and speaks to the depth of information that is relayed and processed during each interaction we have[1].

The depth, breadth, intensity and duration of emotional connections differ widely over time, place, speed of reply, people involved, privacy and method of communication, etc. The 21st century has seen an enormous rise in the use of an ever-increasing variety and availability of long-distance communications — fax, texting, cell phones, interactive social media sites on the internet, etc. This global change has removed the emotional connection from relationships, e.g. intimacy, which used to be tightly linked. (See below, Types and Levels of Intimacy.) This, in turn, has very mixed consequences, as evidence shows that the strength of emotional bonds created between individuals varies depending on the method of communication used[2].

It is always important to remember the power of positive and negative emotional connections. For example, it is well known that students learn best when they have a positive emotional connection to their teacher. Similarly, negative connections encourage more negative results. Think about your childhood and decide how you would like to modify your behavior and resulting emotional connections as you develop as an adult.

c) SEQUENTIAL PROCESS

All relationships begin with establishing an emotional connection of some kind between two people, then they are built by **a sequential process of interactions.** *It is the accumulation of these interactions between people that creates a relationship.* Every action and non-action of both people is permanently woven into the fabric of their relationship because *there are no delete buttons in relationships*. They are repairable but the repairs often show, like darns or patches. Therefore, it is important to develop relationship skills to both prevent damage and to do strong, neat repairs whenever needed. This fabric metaphor is derived from the fact that woven cloth is made from a particular interaction of warp and woof. The warp is composed of all the threads running vertically down the cloth, and the woof/weft weaves across the warp, under then over each warp thread in turn. One person provides the warp and the other the woof of a relationship.

In all cases, each interaction between two people provides a fluid connection, like tossing an invisible ball between the two persons, back and forth. Regardless of how you think of it, this powerful process shapes relationships as surely as the wind from the ocean shapes the trees on the shoreline. The indelible nature of each interaction means that although you can compensate for an error, you cannot undo it.

d) RECIPROCITY

For sustainability, relationships require reciprocity. This means that both parties have to contribute something that the other person values. This is a broader form of "give and take" but it includes the traditional meaning of compromise, with its trade off of concessions. If the giving that builds a relationship is also easy to give, so much the better because that takes less effort to provide. What is easy for you to give?

Sometimes people give only what they wish to give, even if it is emotionally worthless to the receiver, or worse yet, annoying. Yet they usually expect "credit" for their gift. One example is cooking fried chicken to share with someone who is then discovered to be a vegetarian and won't eat it, though they might appreciate the effort. Nonetheless the guest is still hungry! Obviously, better communication skills on both parts would have been helpful in this example.

Reciprocity also requires that the receiver accept gifts, which is very difficult for some people who prefer to give. Such givers are often grateful to find someone willing to accept their one-way giving, especially if there really are no strings attached. Others give without reciprocity — or excessively — to retain a sense of control of the relationship, which may reduce their sense of vulnerability to abandonment, etc.

Sometimes relationships that look like one person is doing all the giving and the other is doing all the taking have a hidden reciprocity. You can only identify such relationships with certainty if the people involved tell you. Occasionally, it is giving without [human] reciprocity to satisfy a religious need. In close knit communities there is often a looser sense of reciprocity: "Pass it on" to someone else in need. This assumes that you will receive from someone when you are in need and later give back to someone else in need within the same community. This works well if the community stays close knit and retains the same values. Can you think of other examples?

e) CONTENT & PROCESS

Many interactions, especially conflicts, are as much about process (how something is done) as they are about content (what was done or said). Common comments when describing an interaction, are, "But that's not how they said it," or "It was the way it went down...," i.e. not what happened (**content**) but how (**process**). "Attitude" relates exclusively to process. In contrast, "He's a nice guy, but nothing gets done" refers to someone who is good at being agreeable, i.e. process, but attends insufficiently to content and action. For success, you have to attend to both process and content, and give both equal attention in any interpersonal transaction, but especially disagreements.

f) MOTIVATION AND IMPACT

It is very important to **distinguish** between **impact** and **motivation** in any interpersonal transaction. Impact is the result of someone's communication/action. Motivation is usually the deliberate intent behind the communication, though someone may be partially unconscious of their motivation. Impact is the **effect** of what you do or say on someone else. It often derives as much from them and their past as it does from your action.

It is a common error to presume impact is identical with motivation (and vice versa). That confusion often leads to unnecessary conflict and distress in relationships. Here's a clear example of the difference. If John is pushed by a crowd and accidentally steps on your toes, they will hurt (Impact). However, it is very unlikely that John *intended* to hurt you (Motivation). Since you cannot always tell by the impact what someone else's motivation was, you often have to deduce it, or ask. Also, do not forget to always pay attention to your impact on other people. When your motivation is unconscious it is occasionally revealed by impact.

g) CONTEXT

Human interactions are very dependent on their context, which means that the same behavior can have different outcomes depending on the setting. For example, **private behavior** can have an entirely different outcome than that same behavior in **certain public settings**. Eating can be private or public, and eating together commonly bonds people. But it is highly doubtful, for example, that crunching carrot sticks during a very formal church service would increase the sense of community. However, doing so with others during the social hour afterwards would likely help to connect people. Can you think of other examples from your life?

In public situations, people tend to be aware of **bystanders as audiences**, and respond to them in different ways. Some will play to their audience, while others will be inhibited from saying what they have in mind. Strangers nearby are often treated as furniture by some people and totally ignored [e.g., when talking loudly about personal matters on the phone], while others will be more circumspect in the presence of strangers than in front of their friends.

There are also wide variations in social responses to public behavior, depending upon the time and place as well as who else is present. Shouting at a ball game is very different from shouting at your coworker. Nudity at a legally designated nude beach is very different from mooning train passengers from a kayak on the Colorado River.

h) PHYSICAL TRANSACTIONS

These are all a type of non-verbal communication, although, they are often accompanied by words, e.g. a handshake. They all require the same attention as verbal communications. Physical communications can either be voluntary (sneering, smiling) or involuntary (trembling, giggling, shivering or flushing). They can be a ritual (hand shake, bow, good-bye wave,); they can be hostile (push, slap, dismissive wave, stab, gunshot); or they can be friendly (a hug, friendly punch, wave or kiss).

Notice that the same behavior can have contradictory meanings depending upon associated factors such as context and process, i.e. how it is communicated.

Physical transactions **may or may not cross social or personal boundaries** or involve **physical contact,** e.g. a blown kiss vs. a real kiss. Certain physical behaviors are **taboo** in U.S. culture, e.g. sexual interactions between parents and children or members of the same family (incest), celibate priests and parishioners (sin), you and your doctor (malpractice) or rape (crime). These taboos and many others in different cultures are crimes punishable by law in each society. What is your personal or family experience with taboos and what have you seen or heard in regards to how such violations of taboos or threats are handled?

i) ETIQUETTE

Interpersonal transactions are usually governed by social rules, called **etiquette.** Etiquette **requires** certain prescribed behaviors. These vary widely between cultures and situations so it is impossible to know them all, though we do learn continuously. It is important therefore, to remember that the rules are always there and, if you do not know them, ask, watch, and learn them. It is always your choice whether or not you follow or break these rules, but the best choices are well informed. The currently controversial practice of being **politically correct** refers to using etiquette designed to reduce unintentional offenses.

> *Conforming* to behavioral etiquette at work will help keep your relationships there smooth and pleasant. In addition, following the etiquette of any situation helps you to quickly figure out what went wrong when you do

have a problem and therefore how to fix it fast. This leaves you **free to do your job** at work as well as you can. It will also help you to minimize trouble in your friendships.

> ➢ *Breaching* etiquette immediately sets up problems that frequently interfere with your performance or distract you. This may be because it causes **tension** in those around you who are aware of the breach or your breach may have the deliberate or unintentional impact of insult or defiance. Obviously, it is therefore important to quickly learn the etiquette of any new organization or situation (ask if it is not clear) so that any breaches are intentional and the consequences are therefore more predictable and manageable.

For example, **Classroom Etiquette,** with which everyone is familiar and which is often used in work meetings includes:

1) sitting still
2) listening silently, striving to understand as much as you can
3) questioning in the expected manner at appropriate times *only*
4) commenting as requested when requested, but *only* if invited/accepted
5) respecting, considering and responding to your fellow students' needs
6) obeying the teacher's instructions
7) conforming to demands e.g. homework done and turned in on time
8) complaining or objecting in the approved manner only

j) POWER DYNAMICS: HIERARCHICAL and COLLABORATIVE

A relationship is **hierarchical** if there is a difference in power between the two people involved. In any situation, it is important to determine if the relationship you are in is hierarchical. If so, you need to understand what the power differentials are, and where they lie. Otherwise, you can be misled into a more passive role than your own power requires or perhaps an inflated view of your power that will trigger interpersonal difficulties that could be avoided with the appropriate deference. These differences in power may be overt, as in the military where everyone's rank is clearly defined, explicit, and worn on their clothing, which inform anyone they meet anywhere. Alternatively, the lines of authority may be deliberately blurred as in some health care teams in hospitals or clinics where collaboration is vital for best performance. However, if you look at who has the last word — who controls the money, who hires and who has the ultimate responsibility for errors or praise for successes — that is usually where the most power lies.

Certain civilian groups, like teachers and employers, have considerable power over their students' and employees' success, and usually fight hard to retain that power. In response, unions are formed to increase the power of their members and limit the power of management or administration. Parenting is another relationship with a power differential: adults in charge and responsible and minor children subordinate. Regrettably, some parents have abdicated their power or it has been usurped, often to the child's detriment. For example, a divorced parent may feel it is too much of a struggle and so unpleasant to arrange regular visits with their child that they stop seeing their child and abdicate that part of their parental responsibilities to the other parent.

Collaboration is when people work together as equals, often with varied backgrounds and widely different expertise and skills. Families who do their chores together demonstrate this concept all the time, each contributing what they are able, which is excellent training for work collaborations.

At work and at home such collaborations require the participants to be able to move comfortably back and forth between feeling competent to exercise leadership when dealing with some aspect they know well and feeling out of their depth and subordinating themselves to another person's expertise. Such work teams have been shown to function best when at least one member of the team is emotionally competent. Why do you think that is? Is this true of your family?

From time to time, even enemies e.g. political, can collaborate in constructive ways and research shows that sometimes the only resolution for various feuds is through collaboration on a shared project. The cute term "frenemy" describes these mixed relationships!

k) THE SOCIAL FORCE

The Social Force, is a type of invisible force field that affects and binds a group of people through shared sensations and creates an intense feeling of connection. Depending on the group's size and make-up, this force has unique effects on the dynamics of the group and impacts the thinking, emotions and beliefs of individual group-members. These effects can be both positive and negative, and often operate outside of the awareness of group-members. It is important to pay attention and bring to conscious awareness how this force impacts you and the groups you belong to as you plan your actions – keeping both your individual goals and the group's goals in mind.

Some aspects of the **Social Force** Include[3]:

> ➤ *The need to perform and the desire to fit in* — In order to foster feelings of harmony and to be seen in a positive light by others in a group we often adapt the ways in which we behave in order to get things done. Effective groups need a healthy level of harmony and respect for the group to function, however, this ideally will not come at the cost of efficiently and candidly sharing valuable ideas. Also, a desire to fit in and a fear of being rejected from the group can influence our ability to think independently and critically, and can reduce our comfort in sharing ideas that may vary with the groups that we are in. An example of this is *Groupthink*. **Groupthink** is a psychological phenomenon that occurs within a group of people in which the desire for harmony or conformity in the group results in an irrational or dysfunctional decision-making outcome. Group members try to minimize conflict and reach a consensus decision without critical evaluation of alternative viewpoints by actively suppressing dissenting viewpoints, and by isolating themselves from outside influences. When groupthink occurs, individuals avoid raising controversial issues or alternative solutions to problems– this results in a loss of individual creativity, uniqueness and independent thinking.

> *Emotional Contagion* – All of us pick up on the emotional-tones of the groups that we belong to – this often occurs outside of our awareness. Although each group member contributes to this emotional-tone, leaders of groups most often have the largest impact on the emotional-tone of groups. This emotional-tone can be subtle, like with certain Organizational Cultures, or very apparent, like the spread of panic in a crowd causing a Stampede. What is the tone of a group you are working with? Are you a leader in such a group? Is there a way to suffuse the group with productive emotions? Most effective groups are suffused with emotions that enhance the confidence and focus of its members.

> *Heightened Feelings of Safety* — Being in particular groups may make us feel shielded from accountability. Also, if 1) a group lacks diversity in intellectual scope and 2) group members lack experience, then there may not be enough lines-of-perspectives to make informed choices. This, coupled with groupthink, can create a troubling combination –making a group overly optimistic about poorly devised plans.

> **Outgroups (or Group Enemies)** – The ingroup includes all the individuals who belong to the specific group that you are a member of — the outgroup includes all the individuals who do not belong to the specific group that you are a member of. Having a clearly defined outgroup may sometimes help to tighten unity amongst ingroup members, however, this can also heighten crude and oversimplified ways of thinking about those outside of the group. Taken to an extreme this can result in irrational and dehumanizing actions against others.

> *Group Factions* – Factions are subgroups that may form within a group – this often occurs once groups become large in size. If factions within a group become strong enough, the faction's members may start to give precedence to its interests over that of the greater group. When this occurs, groups become like "wild horses going in separate directions" – this makes it difficult to achieve shared goals. For more efficient group functioning, it is more effective for group members to focus on areas of common interest,

agreement, and shared purpose (see the Conflict Resolution section later in this chapter for more details).

Three vital components to effective group functioning include:

1) Having a clear sense of **purpose**

2) Having clear **goals** (e.g., to get particular things done, to make particular things, to solve particular problems, etc..,.)

3) Having clear **roles** for group members

Working in a dysfunctional group can have a negative impact on our health and ability to function. The opposite is also true — working in a highly-functioning, emotionally competent group can have a positive impact on us — we can experience the deep satisfaction of cooperating at a high-level and sharing in success with others. We also experience greater empathy, and gain individual and group confidence by working in such groups. One of the goals of becoming more emotionally competent is to create as many such groups as possible – improving and strengthening our families, workplaces, communities and the entire world in the process!

II) FACETS OF RELATIONSHIPS

a) TYPE and LEVEL OF INTIMACY

One of the most important skills in managing a relationship is an awareness of the **type and level of intimacy** or emotional connection that actually exists between you and the other person. Coworkers represent one type of relationship. Some people never develop personal friendships from coworkers, regardless of how close they may seem to be to their coworkers during work hours. They keep their work relationships strictly to one type. In contrast, a change from friendship to lovers — or the reverse — is a change in type and level of intimacy.

The actual level of intimacy you have in a relationship may be very different from the one you wish to achieve — either more or less. If so, you can decide the level and kind of intimacy you desire with this person and make the effort required to **achieve** and **maintain** your preference. We suggest that you begin at the lowest level of intimacy that you are certain is mutual, and proceed from there. Always respect the other person's desires, especially if they wish less intimacy than you or a different kind.

A common conflict in the level of intimacy between two people is that one person wants more contact than the other. If you are unsure how the other person perceives you, you can ask, or use the social etiquette of the time and place. Etiquette is there to facilitate common situations exactly like these, such as unexpectedly meeting someone that you have seen only once or twice before. Obviously, transactions become exponentially more complicated when you are relating to a number of different people at varying degrees and types of intimacy at the same time. Can you think of an example? Remember, usually it can be done, with charm and grace. We hope you will aim for that level of skill in your repertoire.

Although we are focusing on simpler relationships in this section, it is important to note that soldiers, spies and even competitive athletes must have paradoxically intimate and competitive, hostile or destructive relationships with their enemies or opponents. As the stakes rise to life and death, the associated feelings are particularly difficult to manage.

One of the profound impacts of social media is that it has **disconnected intimate content** exchanges — verbal and photographs — **from both emotional connection and physical presence**. There is now electronic-to-electronic (e-t-e) written/verbal or photographic/picture contact, voice-to-voice (v-t-v) contact and person-to-person (p-t-p) contact where one person is actually in the presence of another person. As a result, two strangers may have a detailed electronic exchange about highly personal information in a remote way. When the content is extremely intimate, the two may expect to *feel* intimate and even believe that they are. This includes another aspect of modern life, the wider prevalence in the U.S. of sexuality at a distance (i.e. electronic or multiple physical sexual transactions), with the flimsiest of emotional connections and frequently transacted while intoxicated — which is another obstacle to intimacy.

Sadly, a large number of people have so little actual person-to-person intimacy in their lives that they believe this e-t-e or v-t-v emotional connection is all there is to intimacy. Such distance may also feel safer, and so may even be preferred. But like many other things, what you get out of emotional connections is proportional to what you put in. Those accustomed to real p-t-p intimacy are acutely aware of the dilute nature of electronic or voice exchanges, disconnected from the richer intimacy that comes with the nuances of nonverbal and other rich connections present in p-t-p intimacy. Even the term "face-time" implies an unawareness of the deeper emotional intimacy possible in another's presence. One may begin to wonder if some people's lack of knowledge about deeper levels of intimacy may be a factor behind the casual but dangerous total exposures of other people — often acquaintances, peers or even friends — with devastating impacts.

Since the emotional connection of electronic exchanges is just a thin thread of what is possible person-to-person, it is not surprising that it frequently doesn't survive a person-to-person meeting of strangers. Reconciling our complexity with another person is a complicated business that only happens in reality — person-to-person — not virtually. Those who have used dating websites successfully know to wait and see what the face-to-face meeting reveals, regardless of how well the match looks electronically. It might work as a p-t-p relationship, but many do not.

Once a real intimacy is created in reality within an open and authentic relationship, it can often be well maintained over time and distance with e-t-e or v-t-v connections. Nonetheless, the relationship will need to be "refreshed" periodically with f-t-f to survive with its rich intimacy intact over the long term. A high level of emotional competence is often required to maintain a long-distance relationship as more than "a place holder."

b) BOUNDARIES

Each person has a **physical** and an **emotional boundary,** which they like to control: they prefer to **regulate who and what crosses it and when and where** it is crossed. Infants need to be practically merged with their parents in order to be cared for adequately, so that an infant's boundaries are rarely visible. By contrast, their boundaries are very noticeable when they start to scream because a stranger holds them. Have you ever seen this happen? Gradually as children mature, they become clearer about their boundaries. Think about your own development in this regard. What do you remember?

Structures and family rules often help protect each individual's boundary, e.g. closed doors for privacy. Of course, there are wide variations in intimacy and the treatment of boundaries within families, from nuclear family to extended family, and between genders, etc. It is these rules that we take with us to relationships in the outside world, for better and worse. Think about the range of boundaries in your family and how your use of them may be impacting certain interactions in your life now. It is usually fine to cross boundaries with permission. However, crossing personal boundaries without permission is frequently experienced very negatively, as a boundary violation.

c) VULNERABILITY

Vulnerability is the feeling that you have when you think, "I could get hurt here!" You feel vulnerable to some kind of injury, sometimes *physical* but often *social* or *emotional*, e.g. hurt feelings, rejection, insult, embarrassment, and failure. There is also *political*, *spiritual* and *moral* vulnerability and we'll talk about those three aspects in Step IV: Self-Responsibility. You feel vulnerable when you fear you are going to be attacked somehow and that you might not be able to completely protect yourself.

Soldiers and football players wear helmets and padding to reduce physical vulnerability and athletes also work out not only for superior performance but also because conditioning reduces vulnerability to injuries. Many teenagers fear being talked about, a social vulnerability, and you have to learn how to manage these feelings constructively. Which of these types of vulnerabilities concern you?

As a young child, your parents were responsible for protecting you from the world, including other people. This is what Carl C. Bell, MD[4] calls, "establishing an adult protective shield." After 18, you have to manage that protection for yourself, though family, friends, and others often help you. This responsibility can be quite scary and teenagers and adults often handle this fear by pretending they are not afraid. In fact, at times, you can pretend so well that you completely deny not only the fear, but also the danger itself. Then you can go from feeling worried or even tough enough to handle this situation, to actually feeling invulnerable. That is a very dangerous state because no one is ever invulnerable. When people feel invulnerable, or want to *ward off feeling vulnerable*, they often take unnecessary risks and can get hurt or even killed *without ever consciously deciding whether or not the risk is worth their life*. Think of how you handle your vulnerability in different situations. Use the ten steps of Feeling Management to manage your vulnerability.

d) INSTITUTIONAL RELATIONSHIPS

Common institutional relationships include those with the IRS, your car and health insurance companies, your bank or stock broker, your church, temple or mosque, and your health care providers, etc. Schools and workplaces are the most frequently encountered settings for institutional relationships and include student-teacher, staff-manager, and parent-teacher, janitor-security guard, etc. Such relationships may be hierarchical or collaborative or both, and unions (an institution within an institution) affect the etiquette of many relationships. The separation of church and state is an attempt to simplify the possible number of conflicts that could occur daily if these institutions were overlapping. What institutional relationships do you have in your life? Are any of them the result of having a partner or children?

Institutional relationships often affect people's success in work and education etc. In every work situation, your supervisor judges your performance, and teachers evaluate students, etc. If the superiors are also a mentor they will help you devise ways to sustain your good performance and improve inadequacies/overcome challenges. You will need to recognize each type of institutional relationship you have and use clear, appropriate, courteous communications for skillful management to maximize the net gain you can obtain from each relationship. Don't forget reciprocity.

It is important to know others' agendas — as well as your own — to benefit mutually from these business relationships, which is their true purpose. Such agendas can include promoting learning (e.g. study sessions), fulfilling project or personal needs (e.g. getting a ride to school), setting limits (e.g. "let's leave early and get an early start tomorrow morning"), mutual support (e.g. talking through problems, preventive healthcare), facilitating self-reliance (e.g. " If you can write a draft today, I'll read it over for you"), and managing distance as your paths diverge (e.g. when someone is transferred or decides to stay when you need or wish to leave).

e) FAMILY RELATIONSHIPS

Contemporary families exhibit considerable diversity in their make-up. In addition, many adults have at least one other adult with whom they share some responsibilities for a child, whether or not they are biologically related. For example, count the children in whose lives you have participated. To keep the relationships running smoothly as well as managing the general issues of life that come up in family activities, everyone has to continually employ their relationship skills — especially communication and feeling management skills. The holiday season is notorious for taxing people's skills to the limit in this regard! How does it feel to recognize that you also have to continually maintain every one of these important relationships in order to keep them working well for you?

SKILLS

> **One golden key to skill development is practice, practice, practice**

Now that you have some background in the basics of relationships and have begun to explore some common facets, let's take a look at essential skills and strategies for managing relationships on a daily basis. Once the fundamental skills of getting along in the world have been mastered, people usually do their relationship transactions automatically. They only pay close attention when it is particularly important to them or when a difficulty arises and troubleshooting is required to resolve it. This means that it may look very complicated now, but that it will become easier as you practice the skills required and the steps become familiar. In time, these skills can become as automatic as walking!

I) SETTING GOALS

In order to gain satisfaction in your relationships, your first job is to **decide your goal for this relationship** or this interaction. For instance, what you want from this conversation? Why are you getting together — from your point of view? For example, do you wish to get to know this person because you are looking for a new friend or are you merely passing the time of day? Are you just joking around, relaxing for a few minutes until you have to get back to work? Do you want a favor? Are you using the interaction to show off or model something to a third person? Whatever your goal — long or short-term — if you always use it to guide your behavior, you are more likely to reach that goal.

A goal for a new relationship is not the same thing as an expectation. Your goal is more of a hope because you have no right to expect anything from someone that they have not promised you. And remember, your goal is only one third of the equation. You must then assess what you know about the other person's agenda and learn as much as you can. If their goals are in conflict with yours, this relationship is unlikely to go beyond the superficial level without drama. How can you tell another person's agenda? Look at how your two agendas mesh or clash. Consider how best to handle this.

Finally assess what is happening between the two of you in the here and now. "What you see is what you get" is often accurate. There are more details about this under transactions, later in this section.

II) MULTITASKING IN RELATIONSHIPS

Multitasking is doing two or more things simultaneously. It is an essential skill for the complicated process of developing and maintaining good relationships — with their three moving parts. To support this skill, it is useful to develop the habit of memorizing facts as you listen, read or discuss information in conversation or meetings. This skill is called **quick learning**; it allows you to learn while simultaneously listening and discussing.

You may already be quite skilled in this area, but further practice and application in your relationships can refine your techniques so that you use them automatically without thinking. This reserves time for more complicated and creative tasks, and permits you to **learn large amounts quickly.** This is essential, not only for good work performance, but also to manage the complicated barrage of information and nuances that you experience in every interaction between you and others.

Look back at any new words or concepts you have seen in the framework so far. Repeat them silently to yourself a couple of times, and be sure that you understand them and clarify anything you don't understand. Begin to practice skills now. *Write* the key words and ideas down in your journal or notebook. Ask any questions you need to ask at the appropriate times. *Check your accuracy.*

III) COMMUNICATION

As you read earlier in Step I: Self-Awareness, communication can be verbal or non-verbal. To be effective you must manage your **thoughts, feelings,** physical **actions, voice** and **speech** to accurately convey what you intend but only what you intend to convey. **Conversation** is the most frequently used kind of communication — and these days — text messages, email and similar electronic "conversations" are included in this group. In the past it would have included letters. Face-to-face conversation provides a simple model of interpersonal interaction that helps you develop your skills in **relationship management** in general.

Verbal communication skills include:

a) controlled *behavior* to send precisely the message(s) you intend

b) manage your *feelings*, to control their expression

c) clarity and specificity: choose words carefully for *what* you wish to say

d) modulate *how* you say it to control the tone of the communication

e) schedule *when* you say it for appropriate timing

f) select *where* you say it

g) choose your context for saying it

Careful thought before speaking will allow you to say almost everything you need to say — though not necessarily everything you *want* to say. Many people compromise their integrity with unnecessary lies because they have not developed the tact, diplomacy or charm, to stick to the truth. What you want to say is the place to start — internally or in your journal. Journaling will give you a clear view of the feelings that you are experiencing and the associated facts. It is important to express both in some *appropriate* way that will help you reach your goal in the interaction. Use the feeling management steps to decide on your actual words and phrasing before you speak in tricky situations.

Conversations also involve lots of place specific etiquette. The old phrase **"keep the conversational ball rolling"** refers to the process of back-and-forth in a conversation. It assumes the etiquette which requires that all the people present in the social group at the moment are included and given an opportunity to speak. This, of course, requires that everyone listens the rest of the time, so that no one person "dominates the airspace". This is reciprocity in action. It also means that individuals should both "transmit" and "receive." Therefore, habitual talkers need to learn to switch on and off, and not just walk away when they have finished transmitting. Similarly, silent participants need to learn to speak up occasionally and not leave others to shoulder all the responsibility for an enjoyable conversation.

IV) *OTHER AWARENESS*

After you have a good understanding of your own role in an interpersonal transaction, you are ready to look at your awareness of others. In any interaction, you have to look at both the impact on the other person of what you do and say, and then their response. These two are closely tied together because you frequently have to deduce the impact from the response. It is hard enough at times to know what impact you yourself are feeling from others! But it is often even harder to recognize your impact on others. **Empathy and compassion help** but they are neither always foolproof nor possible. Since you are not inside the other person you can never be entirely sure of the impact of your actions and words and they may not even consciously know. Therefore, you must rely on the other person or someone else to "tell" you the impact of what you say and do.

Misjudgments are common, so be prepared to see them and adjust accordingly without a lot of fuss. Respecting everyone else's *right* to their perspective is crucial in this regard. Even if you are certain they are wrong, you can maintain your integrity and deal with them appropriately if you respect their right to be in error. Also, it is helpful to acknowledge your own errors with a quick, "Oh I'm sorry, I misunderstood. So, what you are saying is…". If the other person is in error you can help them adjust smoothly with, "Oh, I think you misunderstood me. What I meant was….". An angry, "That's not what I said!" is likely to escalate the conflict, even if — or especially if — it is true.

It is also important to recognize that others' skills can affect yours. It is much easier to deal with someone who is interpersonally skilled than someone who is unintentionally or unnecessarily rude or abrasive. Anger is infectious and can tempt you to lose your temper and abandon your skills for a nasty spat instead of staying focused on your original goal for the interaction. When more than two people are involved in an interaction, either as participants or observers, it becomes more complicated. The number of transactions happening at one time, in multiple directions too, increases especially the nonverbal and inaudible asides. However, if you remember that each interaction is built of the same basic steps, it will help you sort them out. For practice, role-playing a current situation while consciously using these steps often helps you clarify your strengths and challenges in talking to people. It is a very effective way to improve your skills and empower you to say whatever you wish to say, (and *not* say what you *don't* want/need to say) appropriately.

V) OBSERVATION

Close observation includes noting your impact on others and gathering missing information. You can then use this information to perform a rapid analysis of what happened before you construct a response designed to meet your goals for the interaction. The steps are:

1. **Watch** the person for indications and signs of what the impact has been. Non-verbal communication, both voluntary and involuntary, is helpful here.
2. **Listen** to what the other person says spontaneously in response, which often includes their reaction.
3. **Assess** the meaning of what is said because people use words differently.
4. **Ask** how they **felt,** or what they **thought.**
5. **Observe** others' responses and use them as ancillary evidence.
6. **Feel** the atmosphere between you and the other person.

VI) RELATIONSHIP MAINTENANCE

As we discussed above in Basics of Relationships, the most viable relationships are reciprocal, where each person benefits by getting some needs met at a price each can afford. That "price" can be paid in an infinite variety of "coin" e.g. attention, services, listening, favors, and gifts. With this in mind, maintenance principles are pretty simple and the skills are all ways to maintain mutually satisfying reciprocity. The challenge is in the "mutual." All relationships take work and they are most rewarding when that work is a pleasure. However, if you have some relationships that don't take work, you can assume the other person is doing more than their share! Check it out and beware the interest and penalties that usually accrue if you rely on that for too long.

Always check regularly whether or not you have given as much as you have taken recently. Then, as needed, correct that balance. You may need to take less of some things or you may need to give more—or both. Secondly, notice and attend to any tensions or difficulties as soon as possible, using the skills in this section.

Mismatched relationships can take more work than well matched relationships and, as a result, they destruct or fade more quickly with neglect. No relationship is a "perfect" match so it is also important to recognize wide differences, e.g. maintenance levels. For example, look at the frequency of contact you and the other person expects. Do you know whether you are perceived as high or low maintenance in each of your relationships? Since everyone is unique, find out early on in your relationships what three things the other people consider most important in a relationship like the two of you have. This is an application of the Self-Assessment Diversity Paradigms from Step I: Self-Awareness — are you a match or a mismatch in these regards?

PRACTICE: 5-STEPS TO PROCESSING AN INTERACTION

Processing an interaction, e.g. a conversation, is complicated. It means understanding your conversation with someone as it unfolds. It is done by repeating five major steps: your action, your impact, the other person's response, the impact of that on you, and back to your reaction, and so on. Here are the details.

Step 1 — Your side of the conversational interaction:
- **Focus:** Be aware of yourself and your **goal** as you speak.
- **Etiquette:** Are you **conforming or breaching? Whose?**
- **Content:** Is **what** you are saying easy or hard to hear? Phrase accordingly.
- **Process: How** are you saying it, e.g. kindly, timidly, incoherently or angrily?
- **Context:** Is this a good **place** or a bad **time** to say it?

Step 2 — Other Awareness:
- Assess **your impact** on the other person: did they understand you?
- Assess **their motivation.**
- **Listen, Observe and Feel** process and content.
- **Read the cues** continuously throughout steps 3- 5.

Step 3 — After the other person responds or reacts:
- Clarify you understood what they said, i.e. **the content,** especially if you have questions or doubts that you heard correctly/or that they would actually say what you think you heard.
- **Ask** how **they feel:** is there a match with the situation?

Step 4 — Feeling Management, at High Speed: (Part I: Self-Awareness)
- **Time out.**
- **Analyze** what happened.
- **Emotions:** Name, Sort and Face your feelings.
- **Choose the best result** for now and later. Remember the goal of your interaction.
- **Plan (Think and Decide)** what to say next, and how to say it etc. to get this result.

Step 5 — Reply or Respond
- **Answer.** Do and say *only* what you decided.
- Back to step 2, until the interaction is over, and you say some kind of **good-bye.**

VII) CONFLICT RESOLUTION

Disagreements are part of human relationships. They can result from genuine differences of point of view, but all too frequently are the result of misunderstandings or poor process skills. You will need the capacity to manage a wide variety of conflicts and disagreements if you are to succeed in life and not become known as argumentative, moody or difficult. If you are good at conflict resolution, it will help you enormously in school and/or work and in every other aspect of your life. People with particularly poor conflict resolution skills can become isolated and lonely, losing friend after friend. Remember that resolution does not always mean agreement. Just as important is a **cordial or respectful agreement to disagree**, which permits you both to cooperate on other areas of agreement or shared purpose.

Transgressions, real or perceived, are particularly difficult to resolve. This is because they involve an injured party and often require some kind of restitution or reparations/compensation for the loss in order to restore goodwill in the relationship. If you broke a promise to return something promptly, an apology and returning it might be enough to restore goodwill. However, you may have irreparably damaged trust and thereby reduce your capacity to borrow in the future. So, keep this notion in mind when you consider violating an agreement.

Forgiveness is not a right and it is not uncommon for severe transgressions to disrupt a relationship permanently. Such one-sided terminations must be completely grieved (see Step II: Self-Development — Grief). It is a missed opportunity for learning and growth if you stop at the protest stage of grief and just vent distress and blame the (originally) injured party, as if *you* are merely an innocent victim of their unreasonableness. Look at your own role, and understand your misjudgment of the other person's feelings, values and perhaps irreconcilable differences (see Step I: Self-Awareness — Diversity).

Negotiating win/win outcomes with other people is an ideal resolution for conflicts. Needless to say, it is not always possible. However, it is partially possible far more times than most people realize. Unskilled negotiators tend to get into competitive interactions that require a winner and a loser quite unnecessarily. Keep this foremost in your mind whenever a disagreement arises in any relationship from storekeepers to coworkers and administrators.

VIII) LIMIT SETTING IN RELATIONSHIPS

One of the most common causes of difficulty in relationships is the complexity involved in determining how much energy to invest in a particular relationship, what form it should take and for which reasons. This is known as **limit setting**, and many people fail to recognize their need for it until they have over invested and feel distressed in some way, often because there is inadequate **reciprocity**. They may feel used or abused, misled, disappointed or enraged.

Prevention is the most effective approach to correcting such situations. This requires you to evaluate every relationship periodically to check if it is in fact satisfying and worth the energy you put into it. That worth can be measured in many forms. At work, your salary is a major portion of your return on relationships. Making friends at work is a bonus. However, if the job you do is especially unrewarding and poorly paid, then your work friendships or coworkers may actually be a major part of the worth of your job. Whenever your situation adds up to a negative, then it is time for you to consider setting some limits and plan how to make some changes (see Step I: Self-Awareness — Feeling Management).

Families and workplaces both provide opportunities for practicing your limit setting skills! The demands that other individuals feel entitled to make on you can exceed your ability or desire to meet them, or vice versa. Sometimes spouses or siblings can be quite clear about setting limits on each other. However, it is common for demands and limits to be poorly articulated in relationships. This can lead to extremely strong feelings of uneasiness, betrayal, abuse and exploitation, respectively. Again, prevention is your best bet. Use your feeling management and communication skills (from Step I: Self-Awareness) to help you respond effectively within these relationships as soon as you suspect there is a problem. There will be more discussion about limit setting in Step IV: Self-Responsibility.

Within hierarchical relationships, setting limits by either party requires especially good skills to not engender resentment. Parents and teachers are often setting limits on children's behavior. With younger children, time-outs and grounding are both limit setting behaviors enforced by an adult who is making the necessary effort to teach the child feeling and behavior management. Teenagers are also known to try to manage up, setting limits on overprotective parents.

IX) GOOD-BYES (TERMINATION)

Satisfying good-byes take practice but they make moving on much easier and less stressful, which is a very useful skill. **Goodnights** between people, e.g. family members, who will see each other in the morning are in fact mini-good-byes. Larger issues are unlikely to be resolved at a goodnight or a good-bye. Don't try. They are best handled earlier in the day, or postponed till the next day. Occasionally, you can settle something simple, for instance, decide when/where you will meet again, or apologize for an earlier remark that you're worried was offensive. It is helpful to use the time immediately after a goodnight or a short-term good-bye to practice processing whatever loss and/or relief you feel at even this temporary **separation**.

Complete farewells, prior to a permanent or long separation have at least four steps: **acknowledgment** it is happening, **review** of the good and bad shared experiences (including the residual feelings), **wrapping-up of loose ends** one way or another, and **acknowledgment of the impact** of the relationship.

English does not make a linguistic distinction between temporary and permanent good-byes. However, the best results come from a frank acknowledgment of the actual expectation of meeting again. Also, just **acknowledge any unfinished business** that remains and will continue unresolved. It often helps to express your feelings — tactfully — about those aspects of the relationship too. Good-byes also require you to assess what impact the relationship has had on you and what changes you may have made as a consequence of being in this relationship. You often carry some parts of a relationship with you, independent of seeing the person again. You may or may not choose to share this with the person from whom you are parting. Thus, good-bye begins yet another round of the **Feeling Management** process (see Part I: Self-Awareness). This feeling management process involves some level of **grief** (see Part II: Self-Development), and facilitates both accepting the loss and also **integrating** and storing whatever happened within the relationship into your "experience file" and treasuring the best of it.

Use your **journal before the final meeting** to increase your satisfaction in your good-byes. On the next page is a check list for reference when planning a good-bye. It can be used when leaving school, ending a relationship, retiring or even at a memorial service.

PRACTICE: GOOD-BYE CHECKLIST

Every complete good-bye to someone has a number of parts:

Non-Verbal:
1. Decide how you wish to physically express your feelings at parting, e.g. a handshake, a pat, a hug, a kiss (what sort?) etc.
2. Quick check of relationship basics & facets if this is OK in the circumstances; adapt if necessary

Verbal:
3. Acknowledge that you are parting
4. Say if you expect to meet again, i.e. good-bye forever or for now, or uncertain
5. Mention the good experiences you shared (highlights only)
6. Mention the bad experiences you shared (highlights only)
7. Wrap up loose ends
8. Acknowledge any unfinished business that remains and will continue unresolved
9. Mention what impact the relationship has had on you including any changes in you from knowing this person
10. Mention what you will take with you and treasure
11. Tactfully express your feelings about the relationship as you part
12. Check if your planned physical expression is mutually agreeable — if necessary

Good-byes are not the time to:

a) Pretend it is not happening
b) Pretend it is temporary when you know it is for a long time and maybe forever
c) Try and resolve something that you have not been able to resolve before
d) Unload lots of negative feelings you never mentioned before

Before & After a good-bye:

1. Use your **journal before the final meeting** to increase your satisfaction in your good-byes
2. Practice recognizing and managing the feelings you have, e.g., loss and/or relief
3. Journal afterwards about how it went: what went well, what went badly

SUMMARY

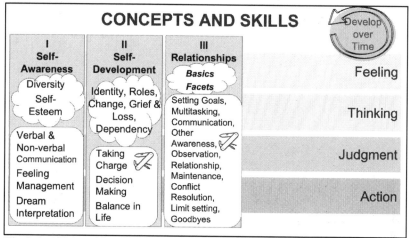

Fig. 3. 1 *Addition of Step III: Relationships Concepts and Skills.*

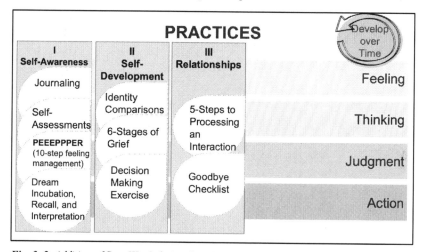

Fig. 3. 2 *Addition of Step III: Relationships Practices*

REFERENCES

[1]Goleman, D. (2006). *Social Intelligence: The New Science of Human Relationships.* New York, NY: Bantam Books.

[2]Sherman, L. E., Michikyan, M., & Greenfield, P. M. (2013). The Effects of Text, Audio, Video, and In-person Communication on Bonding Between Friends. *Cyberpsychology: Journal of Psychosocial Research on Cyberspace, 7*(2), article 3.

[3]Greene, R. (2018). The Laws of Human Nature. New York, NY: Penguin Random House.

[4]Bell CC, Flay B, Paikoff R. (2002). *Strategies for Health Behavioral Change.* In: Chunn J.C. (eds) *The Health Behavioral Change Imperative: Theory, Education, and Practice in Diverse Populations.* New York, NY: Kluwer Academic/Plenum Publishers.

STEP IV

SELF-RESPONSIBILITY

VALUES & JUDGMENT

PHYSICAL and MENTAL HEALTH & SPRITUALITY

LIFE STYLE

AUTONOMY

SELF RELIANCE   **PLANS & STRUCTURE**

SELF ASSESSMENT

LEADERSHIP

JUDGMENT: Good & Bad

SELF-RESPONSIBILITY

INTRODUCTION

Ideally, Self-Responsibility is something that we all come to gradually and to varying degrees. From childhood through your teens, you would be allowed to make increasingly more decisions by yourself, and gradually you'd assume more responsibility for yourself, and perhaps even share responsibility for others. Nonetheless, all that time, most of you had a parent or adult who was more responsible for you than you were for yourself. Though you may have chaffed at their control, this was probably a relief when things got too difficult, or if you just flaked out.

However, at age 18, legally, that responsibility changed hands overnight, whether or not it was acknowledged or acted on in your family. At age 21, you have complete authority over every aspect of your own life, including e.g. drinking and driving. This authority has important implications for your personal development, because it carries with it the *freedom of choice* and all the responsibility for any consequences, good and bad — there are rewards and costs for your actions and inactions.

Maturity is the exercise of a competent level of adult self-responsibility skills. People usually **mature unevenly** and not necessarily in synchrony with the demands of their life. As a result, you may have to develop self-responsibility in some areas and not in others. The latter areas will be your choice. Sometimes circumstance may flip and you may have to take direction in areas where previously you may have been accustomed to autonomy, and so on. Moreover, **maturity also comes in waves,** with lots of receding between the high-water marks, especially when ill or under stress. Take a few minutes to identify the skills you have already developed. This section addresses some of the major contributors to the complexity of managing your own life, and will help you think through your individual issues.

CONCEPTS

VALUES and JUDGMENTS

Many leadership roles, in politics, business, and employment or at home, carry with them an increased access to powerful forces. Forces such as power, money and sex expose leaders to both exciting and dangerous situations. Such situations require you to 1) master the concept of **boundaries** (see Step III: Relationships), and then 2) know and use appropriate values and good judgment, so that you can 3) perform well and achieve your goals with a tranquil state of mind. Each of your actions will be subject to the judgments of others as well as yourself. Therefore, it is important to understand your own attitudes and feelings towards these tremendous forces as you develop as a leader. In addition, learn the values and attitudes of the larger community in which you live and work. Decisions you have seen national leaders make in this regard can serve as teaching examples.

Individuals in America usually have the freedom to decide which values are of importance to them in their personal lives. Those discussed below have relevance to many professions, e.g. technology, business, law and healthcare. All ethical people must adhere to many specified values in their professional life, and be cognizant that the law *prescribes* numerous standards and forbids certain behaviors.

I) INTEGRITY

Integrity includes honesty, and soundness of moral principle. Consider your attitudes and feelings about your various levels of integrity with respect to any number of issues like "white lies," cheating (of all kinds), repaying debts and loans, and competition. Think of incidents you have seen or in which you have participated that raised questions for you in these areas. *Self-awareness*, *decision-making*, *judgment* and *discipline* [more on discipline later in this chapter] are crucial to controlling your actions to conform to your own *values*, despite the immediate pressures of any one situation.

It is helpful to consider the familiar issue of cheating in this light. For example, one can understand a student's rule "Don't snitch" as a **mission** that comes under the **end result desired (ERD)** to *protect other students.* School administration also shares this **ERD** of protecting students. However, with cheating, true (long-term) protection of the student who cheats comes with reporting the cheating, particularly if the administration manages students who cheat in a way that will in fact *protect* the student in the long run from their own poor judgment that led them to cheat. Other students with information about cheating will feel required to **cross boundaries**, though not violate them ("snitch") if they **share the view** of the end result desired. This requires that everyone have confidence that the matter will be handled in the best interest of the student — long and short term — and in the best interest of the educational institution, and ultimately, the country. After all, the country relies on meaningful education standards to function at an optimal level.

The same type of issue can arise in the workplace when supervisors and employees cover-up errors. The 2011 Japanese nuclear reactor disaster and California's PG&E explosions and exposure of known but unaddressed faults in the gas pipelines are examples. It is a basic responsibility of emotionally competent adults to help create an environment where it is easiest for everyone involved to achieve the best result for now and later. These examples indicate how arduous a task this is.

II) PRIVACY

Take time to review your own attitudes and behavior towards privacy, secrecy, and openness, because they will inform your instinctive responses to any number of experiences in life. Begin to develop a conscious code of behavior for yourself and pay attention to differences from your peers in this regard. Discuss with your friends and partner, if you have one, any limits of confidentiality or privacy that you face. Revise your ideas regularly as you face more complexities, and state your views and reasoning explicitly when relevant. Think of your attitudes towards gossip from this perspective.

Social media has now raised this issue to international prominence. It is clear from countless newspaper articles, YouTube videos, and Facebook posts, etc. that millions of adults and children have yet to think through these issues with "the best result for now and later" in mind. The costs of these omissions can be enormous, e.g. suicide. Healthcare, law, journalism and religion are all fields that require and allow a great deal of confidentiality — which is an extension of privacy — by law, custom and human respect. Breaches may occur in these areas, and it helps to be prepared for them if/when they occur.

III) POWER

Power can be very attractive to some people yet very frightening to others. How do you feel about it? The **advantage of power** is that you can use it to get things done. Power can also give deeds a significant impact, whether for good or for ill, even when they produce a neutral or frivolous outcome. The more power you have, the wider and deeper is the impact of what you will be able to do. Thus, small mistakes can be enormously costly, even dangerous. Similarly, small changes for the good can have huge positive ramifications. Power coupled with responsibility and accountability is usually the safest way for it to be exercised. What distinguishes **use** of power from **misuse**?

Influence is a kind of indirect power, which can have a similar effect on outcomes. It often comes with high stature but no authority. When *deciding* to exercise power — which is the main point of seeking it — always look at the costs and benefits ahead of time (see Step II: Self-Development — Decision Making).   These costs commonly affect others more than the person in power, at least initially. Also, keep **impact** in mind, unintended as well as intended consequences (see Step III: Relationships – Processing an Interaction).

Consider your adult feelings about your power and/or powerlessness and compare them to your feelings when you were a child. How do you feel about varying amounts of power, e.g. influence over a friend or co-worker? What do you notice is most tricky for you? Consider your experience of power in your family of origin and as a child in this light. We take these early impressions with us all our life and your awareness of them will help you manage them with emotional competence.

Some jobs or professions and family roles in some cultures have high status if only in that context, e.g. military or corporations. As a result, individuals holding those positions have automatic power and Influence that cannot be disregarded by them — though others may choose to do so! In contrast, a suggestion or invitation from them may be received as an "order", which can be equally problematic and can quickly degenerate into a "hostile workplace" or "abuse" situation.

IV) POLITICS

All politics, office or institutional, family or community, local and national, are powerful forces that affect every adult and child within organizations and outside. Although there is an ebb and flow in the focus of politics, they can affect every aspect of our lives from education, safety, war, employment and public health to our values like money, religion, sexuality, reproduction, privacy and ethics. Since the economy is currently a huge social and political issue that affects us all, adults ignore national politics at their own risk these days.

Have you constructed and articulated your own political philosophy that will assist you in your success? Even if you are apolitical — deliberately or passively because you do not like or understand politics — that is a definite political position that affects your life. See if you can explain your stance clearly and watch for any effects it has on your life. Thinking through your politics will also help you position yourself thoughtfully in all your interactions that have political implications or components.

V) MONEY

Everyone has considerable demands on their money, and regardless of how much they have, there are continual decisions to be made about **spending, saving,** or **investing** income. What are your attitudes and feelings about money? How well do you know your money facts? Can you distinguish between **credit** and **cash**; **income** and **assets**; **solvency, debt** and **philanthropy**; **wealth, poverty** and **social class?** Do money issues impact your peace of mind? For some people, money is so important that financial greed dominates their ERD and all their missions in life. Checking your balance in life would warn you if you were on a destructive [rather than a low-income based survival] track. In either case the Feeling Management exercise from Step I: Self-Awareness might help you re-equilibrate.

When you *choose* between savings and optional purchases, such as dinner out, designer clothes or luxury vacations, keep in mind "the best plan for now and later" (See Step I: Self-Awareness — Feeling Management). Remember that social and political power — your family's and that of your community — is closely related to wealth. This means that important later choices may be restricted by lack of savings or available money.

In addition, the need for more money commonly undermines comfort and/or integrity. Does this matter to you? Moreover, debt is a powerful force that can threaten your integrity as well as your survival and is a common cause of homelessness.

For the rest of your life you will have many demands on your money, and constant choices about **spending**, **saving**, or **investing** income. You will be more successful in reaching your financial goals if you are clear about your values about money. For example, higher education is known to cost a great deal of money, and in turn, can provide relatively higher individual incomes in a good job market. This issue should be part of your adult financial decision making.

VI) *SEXUALITY*

Sexual relationships are a highly charged, complex version of interpersonal transaction (see Step III: Relationships – Type and Level of Intimacy). In this overview, we are going to emphasize a few key points. In order to enjoy sexual relationships to the fullest, they require even more learning, skills and experience than other relationships, plus the continual exercise of considerable self-responsibility. For most people, they are worth the price, regardless of what they cost. Handled with emotional competence they can be a wonderful bargain, from consensual flirtation to sensuality and private sexuality within a rewarding relationship!

Unfortunately, these legitimate pleasures have been almost eclipsed by media publicity about people who have trouble with the emotional competence required to manage their sexuality well. There are daily exposures of sexual misconduct from sexual harassment, rape, and unsafe sex, as well as molestation within families and institutions and "sexploitation" in films and advertising. Sex can also become one of the addictions and its overwhelming force field can undermine integrity in the wink of an eye.

Take a moment now to privately recall your own earlier sexual experiences because they affect your attitudes and feelings today. If you have positive associations, they can significantly enhance your sexual relationships and your comfort in discussing such issues where appropriate. If you have had negative encounters, processing your traumatic or negative experiences helps you prevent them from haunting you (see Step I: Self-Awareness — Feeling Management). You are unlikely to forget them, but they will be less likely to spill out of your emotional closet at inconvenient times.

When traumatic sexual incidents are "forgotten" without processing the feelings, the facts may have been repressed to postpone dealing with the feelings until a time when you are better able to handle them. **Psychotherapy** and medication can help with processing the more complicated issues, such as posttraumatic stress (PTSD). If you have had a negative sexual experience — as victim or perpetrator — how do you plan to handle it to minimize its impact on your personal growth?

Review your attitudes, feelings and behavior about sex at present. What is the **relationship between sex and alcohol or drugs** for you? How well do you handle information about differing sexual orientations? What role do you have in addressing responsible sexual behavior? Remember, as an adult, you are responsible for your safe sex and that of your partner – this may include 1) the use of condoms for prevention of both STDs and unwanted pregnancies, and 2) appropriate medical treatments for contraception and/or for sexually transmitted diseases.

The consequences of mixing alcohol or drugs and sex are also your responsibility and they can be lethal socially as well as physically. This is partially because substance use and abuse distorts your judgment and can dissolve discipline and other facets of self-control leaving you vulnerable and powerless to adjust your behavior appropriately to changing circumstances. Use the Self-Assessment Diversity Paradigms in Step I: Self-Awareness to clarify your own **sexual values and boundaries** and compare them to those of others you know.

VII) SPIRITUALITY & RELIGION

Choosing your religion or spiritual practice is an extremely important process internally and externally, even if you decide on none. Religion and spirituality are personal matters for most people, providing internal support and strength that can be enormously important and central to their lives. For some of them it can range from a nonnegotiable requirement for membership in a community, e.g. Amish, to an intermittent practice. Others find religion totally irrelevant to their lives. Still others find spirituality in nature or other experiences that serve a similar function. This area is another example of our human diversity that can be managed with tolerance. How is this topic handled in your family?

Some religious beliefs, such as rituals or observances, proselytizing, superiority, no medical interventions etc., can produce conflict in certain situations. These are usually related to enforcement attempts by one person or group on another. Explore your own belief system with its tolerances and intolerances now, so that you can plan how to manage relationships with people from whom you are likely to differ. If you work for a religious institution or your child attends one, many of these issues will occur regularly, and clarifying boundaries and mutual expectations can be very helpful.

VIII) ETHICS & MORALITY

Ethics are moral principles or rules of conduct that often differ from one culture or religion to another, and in different time periods. Your morality is your degree of conformity with moral principles. A moral person is concerned with the goodness or badness of human character or behavior and/or the distinction between right and wrong. Ethics and morality are sometimes aligned with the law of the land, but not always.

Traditionally, ethics and morality were inextricably linked with religion and taught in religious institutions. However, contemporary connections between religious belief and the daily practice of morality differ widely. This is likely because of a number of factors including tolerance of various religions, agnosticism and atheism. Tolerance in turn led to the separation of church and state in the U.S. and elsewhere, with a corresponding decrease in the enforcement of participation in religious services. More recently the exposure and legal prosecution of cover-ups (e.g. child abuse) and/or open advocacy of crimes (e.g. murder) by religious leaders have eroded the links between their institutions and morality. Regardless of the causes, the burden of understanding moral and ethical issues and operating on moral principles [or not] is shared by every adult. Every family decides what and how to teach and support morality or immorality within their group. What did you learn at home? Have you changed since then?

IX) PHYSICAL and MENTAL HEALTH

Physical health and mental health are inextricably entwined with emotional empowerment and professional success. It is therefore imperative that you maintain your health as well as you can, considering your genetics. It is helpful to think of health care in three categories: **prevention, maintenance, and treatment.**

Prevention includes **safety** (e.g., seat belts, no substance *abuse* and reasonable risk aversion); **adequate sleep** (since many accidents are related to sleep deprivation); **education** (e.g., applying this framework); **flossing your teeth** (at least once daily as dentists recommend); and **Health check-ups** as appropriate – all of these fit under the "stitch in time" rule.

Maintenance includes a **healthy diet** (e.g., low fat, limited sugar, whole grains, high vegetables and fruit, reasonable and adequate portions, no bulimia or starvation); a regular and reasonable amount of **exercise; stress** reduction (since stress reduces resistance to many illnesses and is associated with increased accidents); and **compliance with treatment** programs (including medications and physical therapy exercises recommended to you by competent professionals).

If you are unfortunate enough to have a serious diagnosis, competent medical treatment can often minimize the length of time and the degree to which you are incapacitated from physical or mental illnesses, although regrettably, it can rarely eliminate it. Similarly, appropriate treatment can alleviate your suffering when there is no cure available so that you can continue to maximize your enjoyment of life.

X) LIFE STYLE

Life style is commonly discussed these days as if it were a jacket that you can take on and off at will, or is snatched from you by, for example, a job loss. However, for long-lasting **peace of mind** it also must be firmly grounded in your self-knowledge.

All the issues discussed in this Emotional Competence framework, e.g. feelings, values, ethics, personality, preferences and tastes, etc. are relevant to the development of your life style. Every individual must strive to synthesize these factors into a philosophy of life, in order to create an authentic, satisfying whole life with rewarding, intimate relationships. Everybody's unique synthesis will be reflected in the details of their life style, which includes their work and hobbies. Each of our long list of choices, of friends and life partner(s), if any, children or none, professional situations from primary education to retirement, part-time or full-time work, housing, clothing, travel, time-out or fast-track, etc. are all contributors to our lifestyle.

Only you can decide (see Step II: Self-Development – Decision Making) which choices will give you "the best result for now and later" (see Part I: Self-Awareness — Feeling Management). Formidable social forces pull us towards this fad and that trend, this image and that posture. You will see people every day who appear successful but live their lives in the tension of an inauthentic image, desperately trying to believe the myth that "perception is reality". Sometimes that sham is tolerable only through heavy drinking, or drugs, etc. (This is to be distinguished from the common difficulty of reconciling your old sense of self with genuine success, although this too needs to be emotionally addressed, as do real failures).

Nonetheless, if you allocate some **courage** for developing your Emotional Competence, steadily increasing self-understanding and your proficiency with the Big Four — coordinating *feeling*, *thinking*, *judgment* and *actions* — you have a good chance of making **satisfying choices** for your life, and for the most part, living contentedly with relative peace of mind.

SKILLS

I) AUTONOMY

Autonomy is independence or freedom. It is the freedom to work towards your goals or not, and even to sabotage them. You can, for example, study for your test, watch TV or go on a date; save or spend money; eat health food or eat junk food; tell the truth or lie to someone; go to class or skip it; and get help or go to sleep when you're stuck. Think about your autonomy and anticipate some issues you will face. Where are your strengths with autonomy? Where are your challenges? Where do you see possible pitfalls ahead and how do you plan to deal with them?

a) PARADOX OF FREEDOM

> ➤ **To keep your freedom, control your actions**

The paradox of freedom is that in order to keep your freedom of choice, you have to control your own behavior, constantly using good judgment as you exercise your self-responsibility. Otherwise, you will gradually lose that very same freedom and the power it carries.

b) DISCIPLINE

Discipline is a state of order maintained by training and control. It often involves rules, of course, and you may need to create new ones for yourself to support your chosen career or personal path. Consider your training in discipline and how that affects your current performance. Although this is not a popular skill, it is priceless for productivity and accomplishments. Without it you are totally dependent on — and vulnerable to — others, e.g. faculty, parents, state licensing boards, and the district attorney, forcing things on you. Discipline is invaluable for accomplishing many of the ordinary, boring tasks of life and can be an excellent counter for procrastination. You can support your discipline by **developing routine habits** for many of your chores, e.g. always clean up after you eat *before* you go onto something else or every time you try on three clean outfits and reject them, put all three away *before* you go out.

II) *SELF-RELIANCE*

Self-reliance is a basic skill needed for self-responsibility. It involves being able to take care of yourself — *physically, emotionally* and *spiritually*. Paradoxically, this includes **recognizing when to seek help.** The need for help varies from time to time, and is highest in new learning situations and unfamiliar predicaments. This is another one of those dynamic balances that require you to exercise **good judgment**.

Now, evaluate where you are developmentally at present with regard to self-reliance, looking for anything you would like to change. How self-reliant are you now? Is there a difference between your work and home behavior and why? Where do you find self-reliance easy? Where are you extremely dependent on others to direct you or take care of you? When do you tend to accept responsibility for your life situations or to blame others or attribute your results to luck, good and/or bad? Is this age/situation appropriate or is it irresponsible? Are you *too* responsible? We suspect you can identify where you are developing with regard to self-reliance, where you are stuck, and where you are resting. Can you also tell how much your current developmental level has to do with your family, given what you have seen modeled or has been expected of you? Has fate been a major influence?

It is always helpful to identify what you need to support your self-reliance, relinquish unnecessary or harmful dependencies (see Step II: Self-Development – Grief), and at the same time continue to seek appropriate guidance, direction and constructive support whenever necessary.

INITIATIVE

The dictionary defines initiative is "an introductory act or step, a leading action". Consider some area in your life in which you have already had the opportunity to take initiative, and examine the feelings that these actions have produced in you. What have been the most enjoyable or the hardest? How have you managed them? How do you savor the good feelings?

Where do you find showing initiative easy? What have been the costs of your initiative? Gains? Where do you see the next occasion for you to take initiative coming up? How do you plan to handle it?

III) PLANS and STRUCTURE

Success often rides on well thought out plans and structure. Therefore, it is imperative that you develop plans and structures to manage your autonomy, determine your goals, and stay on course to reach them. This includes taking advantage of your strengths in setting goals and developing plans and structures and also reinforcing and protecting yourself in weaker areas. When you make **informed plans**, you empower yourself for success by doing your homework *ahead of time*. You learn what will be required and therefore, can include this in the plan.

The key to this area of empowerment is to keep your choices and decision **conscious**. Even if you are not thinking of them at the moment, you should be able to access them quickly at any time.

a) GOAL SETTING

Goals come in various shapes and sizes, and satisfaction is usually related to **realistic expectations**. Keep this in mind as you set your goals. Your expectations of yourself may be higher or lower than your family or counselors tell you. This is a good place to practice self-reliance, basing it on emotionally competent self-awareness of your potential. Setting goals is part of the first steps in achieving personal success. You might be successful without a specific goal, but it is less likely. One very effective way to think of **goals** is **in two or three levels**. The **End Result Desired (ERD)** is the highest level or overall goal – it functions as your perpetual, guiding principle and is usually your longest-term goal.

Lower level goals are shorter term **projects,** and even smaller **missions**, intended to help you reach your ERD. When you succeed, you may select a new ERD, and design new missions. For example, in high school or college, becoming an engineer may have been your ERD. Your project was to stay the course long enough and take the right classes to graduate in your major as soon as possible with a diploma or a degree or two. Your mission may have been to get high enough grades in each class to stay eligible for your ERD. After you become an engineer, you have achieved one ERD. So, your **new** *ERD* may be to stabilize your family and your *project* may be to settle in one place so that everyone can develop long-term relationships and a community. Your mission might be to look at various jobs, communities and homes with this in mind. Or you may wish to become internationally respected in your field, and therefore, you and your family will need to travel so that you can achieve that ERD.

Reading this Universal Framework for Life may be part of a mission related to your overall ERD as an individual e.g. success in your professional, personal or family life. Always keep your ERD in sight to maximize your chances of success. Start by thinking about what kind of adult you propose to become. For instance, do you wish to be wealthy or just financially comfortable? An ordinary working person who is relaxed and/or accomplished or a famous, powerful and/or beloved person? Every choice will carry with it certain responsibilities and rewards, i.e., the costs and benefits of that decision (see Step II: Self-Development – Decision Making). Are you willing to pay the prices attached to the benefits you choose? If not, rethink your ERD.

Once your ERD is realistic, ask yourself will it satisfy you? For example, considering your present starting point, can you have a large family and stay at home? Next, look at your second level goals, missions and projects, and see if they are well designed to accomplish — and not deflect you from — your ERD. Rethink your projects and missions if they do not actually move you towards your ERD. *Record* your ERD list in your journal, and the projects and smaller missions that you have set to achieve them. Check back every month to see if you are on track, and make the indicated adjustments and course corrections.

b) TIME MANAGEMENT

This skill is one that will repay you tenfold to learn, even if you have to try repeatedly to master it. Understanding your own process thoroughly helps too. Your realistic plans always need **a timetable**. Be reasonable in your estimates of time, not just fanciful or too optimistic or impractically self-indulgent. Keep your **end result desired (ERD)** in mind too. This is a pragmatic way to move steadily towards your goals and limit any "unforced" delays. Unavoidable delays will then usually come from things you can't control or anticipate. Unfortunately, such things happen to all of us, and the feeling management and grief skills can be very effective in helping us cope. On these occasions, knowing your **priorities** will help you carefully reorganize your plans so that you can avoid the tragedy of reaching only half of your goals, without ever having chosen which half was more important. The more ambitious you are, the further you will have to go. Pace yourself accordingly.

"Back planning" is the technique of concretely calculating back in time from the deadline what has to be done by when, in order to reach your goal by your deadline. It is invaluable for time management. For example, back plan small missions scheduled for one day such as getting a hair-cut, finishing an errand, getting something to eat, getting some exercise, and completing usual routine daily work-obligations. The same back planning skill is essential for larger issues too, like going back to school to switch careers, or finding a partner.

For example, if you want a family you have to consider the number of children you want and the timing. It is usually safer for the babies if the biological Mom is under age 35 and often easier for you and your partner to conceive before Mom is 40 years old. If you wish to finish with childbearing by age 30, you will probably have to start much sooner to accomplish this goal. For success, your plan must take all these considerations into account.

c) ANTICIPATING PROBLEMS

If you remember the section on feeling management (see Step I: Self-Awareness), we considered situations that had already taken place. With serious personal responsibilities, that is rarely enough. You have to look ahead and **anticipate problems** to avoid as many of them as possible. In this way, problem solving can be scheduled and routine, rather than become part of repeated crises that interrupt your daily missions for success.

For predictable problems, you need to design realistic plans that don't cost more than you are able or willing to pay. Similar to the process of decision making (see Step II: Self-Development), whenever you design a plan, assess the **costs and benefits of**

this plan. What is the cost in money, time, leisure, fun, sleep, and relationships — which and in what ways, etc.? Is it worth it? Ask yourself if this cost is realistic. What's more, even if it is realistic, can you afford it? Are you willing and able to pay the cost? If someone else is paying, are they willing? If not, the plan will fail and you will have wasted a lot of time pursuing something that you could have predicted ahead of time would be unsuccessful. Also, allow some flexibility in case fate impacts your plan, as regrettably, it regularly does.

IV) SELF-ASSESSMENT WITHOUT BLAME or EXCUSES

When taking responsibility for yourself, it is essential to take the initiative to **evaluate yourself accurately, honestly — and kindly.** For example, when measuring your achievements, first decide whether you are measuring from the bottom up, as beginners need to be assessed, or from the top down, as one does for experts. If you are a novice at something, a 100% improvement might take you from a 20% F to a 40% F on the expert's scale. This is an impressive accomplishment for a beginner! But if you are an expert in this field, both scores indicate a serious problem. Accuracy requires that these different contexts for the scores be taken into account during your self-evaluation. Honesty requires you to not adjust the scores if you wish to achieve expertise.

High achievers often have trouble with the "kindness" part of self-assessment. If you are in the habit of using harsh criticism to motivate yourself, you should now begin to devise a kinder version of motivation — more carrots and less stick! This kinder version of motivation can take you just as far, perhaps even further, and you will definitely enjoy the journey far more.

Make it a point to look at what your role was in significant events. What was done well? What was poorly done? Were there any contributing factors beyond your control? How crucial were your actions compared to those factors? What initiative do you now need to take to try to fix things? Finally, refer to **Feeling Management** (see Step I: Self-Awareness) to decide what you are actually going to do.

Also, remember when evaluating your satisfaction in a relationship, especially romantic ones, it is important to compare the best times in the relationship with the best times alone, and the worst times similarly. There is always the temptation e.g., to compare the best of one with the worst of another, to justify your emotional position of the moment which is neither accurate nor honest and frequently unkind to both of you.

V) LEADERSHIP

Leadership means very different things to different people. We all need to compose our own definition of leadership and *decide* what role it will play in our lives. If leadership interests you, you will be well served to develop your relationship skills with the variety of people with whom you will be interacting with in your leadership roles throughout your life. Examine your own leadership experiences (including parenting). What do you see? What leadership roles have you accepted to date? Think about the responsibilities you have discharged and those you have dropped/flubbed/bungled. What did you learn about yourself, those you led, and leadership itself? What are your feelings about them? Think about which of your leadership skills need further development.

Remind yourself of some of the adults you know in leadership positions. Did they choose the positions or were they chosen? Think about whom you judge to be a good leader, and who is a poor leader, why? What is a **leadership failure**? Now look at your personal experiences of leaders in your communities, e.g. high school, employment or church, what do you see? Who would you like to emulate? What plans do you have for leadership this year? Remember, any change can be experienced as a loss as well as a gain.

The emotional intelligence skills covered in this framework will help you make the most of your leadership opportunities when they arise. By doing so, your skills may surpass those of many people whom you will meet throughout your life, and it will serve you as well as better than average driving skills on the roads.

What values do you wish to see where you work and play? Do you have a plan to introduce or support them there? Remember, leadership by example is one of the most powerful tools of a leader.

a) COMMUNITY RESPONSIBILITY

The idea of community is familiar to us all, from our own neighborhood and family to the wider community of state or nation or even the world. Each one of us will think of it slightly differently, even if we came from the same place.

As an adult, friends or churches will look to you for community service. You will have to *decide* what, when, where and how much you do. How do you see yourself in relation to the state and the nation? At what level, if any, do you feel an obligation to serve or pay back the privileges you have received? Do you have a global perspective? And if so, where do you feel obligations? Always pay attention to the balance of your own needs, that of your family of origin, and your nuclear family.

The way in which you resolve these issues in community relationships, including family, often determines whether or not you get a reputation for being a "giver" or a "taker" (e.g. as someone who "pulls their weight" or as someone who is unreliable about participating in the common good). It is your responsibility to determine your behavior and to assess how well it matches your values in this area and your view of yourself. It is important to your emotional wellbeing to align these values and view since hypocrisy produces stress. If you can also communicate your positions accurately, simply and courteously (using diplomacy and tact) you will increase the chances that you will be understood by others.

b) LIMIT SETTING

Limit setting is the management of your obligations in a way that allows you to both be successful and have fun. Limits provide the necessary balance to community responsibility. Limiting setting in relationships is a subcategory of this area. Without continual limit setting, it is easy for many people to get overextended, lose sight of their own goals, and as a result, get off track. Let's discuss how you can make the leadership contributions you choose yet discharge your community obligations within safe limits. First, determine your **priorities**. Then check the balance between your contributions to the *community*, *yourself* and your *family*. Then, decide where you are over committed and need limits. Plan how to set them. How difficult will it be to stick to them once you have *decided* where they are? (Remember, *Follow your plan and nothing but your plan*).

Paradoxically, high achievers — with more educational, intellectual and other resources than most people — can need more limit setting, and sooner than many others.

VI) JUDGMENT: GOOD AND BAD

Good judgment is the ability to rank choices from the most constructive to most destructive. It is a complex process essential for success, which has to occur before an action is carried out, or decided against. This process requires you to:

1. **Anticipate** the consequences of the act (or inaction), both the ones you want and the ones you do not want
2. **Evaluate** the **risks of failure**
3. **Evaluate** the **benefits**
4. **Evaluate** the **costs** of the action (or inaction) even if successful
5. **Rank** how likely the negative consequences are compared to the positive
6. **Consider other actions** you might do that increase the chances of your getting the positive consequences, and decrease the chances of the negative consequences
7. **Decide** whether or not to go ahead with your action
8. If action is necessary, make the **best choice**, long and short term

Bad Judgment is the failure to see and distinguish between constructive and destructive choices. It often results from:

1. **Acting impulsively** on strong feelings without reflection
2. **Acting without thinking**, e.g. someone asked you to do it
3. Acting after looking at *only* **the positive** consequences
4. Acting without looking at *all* **the possible negative** consequences
5. Acting, **despite "knowing better,"** i.e. that the negative consequences outweigh the positive
6. **Hoping for the best** without planning for the worst
7. **Not acting when action is necessary** to protect your *best* interests in the long and short term.

STEP V

REFLECTION

and

FEELINGS

MOTIVATION

REFLECTION   **JOURNAL REVIEW**

EMOTIONAL LITERACY

FEELING TRANSITIONS   **COMMON FEELINGS**

INTEGRATED SKILLS PRACTICE

REFLECTION and FEELINGS

INTRODUCTION

Your periodic review of your emotional competence development is a true test of self-responsibility and many of the other skills described in this book! This framework covers an enormous amount of psychological information that will be invaluable for your own personal and career growth and in your role as an adult — *if you use it*. Obviously, no one except you will know if you actually do so — at first. However, if you do use it, your skill level in all three dimensions of emotional competence will be reflected in your career, relationships and life goals as you improve — from coordinating feelings, thinking, judgment and actions ["The Big Four"] for an Instant Response to your Considered Responses using Feeling Management ["PEEEPPPER"] and this fifth step of your personal development.

Above all, **your ultimate satisfaction** in life will be your own measure of success in continually applying this comprehensive approach to emotional intelligence skills to all aspects of your life. Like many things, what you get out of your emotional life will reflect whatever you put into it. Also, remember that your sense of **the congruity of your entire life**, which is increasingly important as we age, depends upon your ability to integrate these skills into your personal and professional development. You will feel more authentic and less like an imposter or a victim as you refine the skills outlined in this syllabus. Gradually, emotionally competent responses will become part of who you are. Moreover, your skills will help others improve theirs as you lead by example.

CONCEPT

MOTIVATION

> **Feelings are the driving force in our lives.**

Whatever we do, it is motivated by feelings. It is often easy to recognize feelings as the power source of someone's behavior, but often hard to identify the particular emotions operating. But keeping the above principle in sight will help you detect the role of feelings more easily.

When we choose to play, it is usually easy to choose something we enjoy, e.g. the beach or a movie, horseback riding or a video game. We also know that we are motivated by the pleasure we derive from the activity and those good feelings can be even greater if we are avoiding a less pleasant occupation. That's an easy one to analyze and understand.

Other actions — or inactions — are more complicated and require reflection to unravel. When we are "forced" to do unpleasant things we are often so resentful about it that our other feelings are often eclipsed by the angry and powerless feelings. We may not even recognize the love that drives us to care for an elderly relative who no longer recognizes us. But if we are doing such family care, we can assume that the love is stronger than the anger, because the loving action is winning — this is called "emotionally voting with your feet", as the predominant (winning) feeling is expressed in our actions (even if we are not consciously aware of it). Sporadic elder abuse sometimes comes from the anger temporarily winning over the love or values, or the conflicting feelings warring, with no clear winner or loser.

Another common example of mixed feelings is that you may be a reliable worker at a job you dislike because you need the money to pay for your expensive car; or you may be desperately saving all that money to feel secure. Alternatively, you may be housecleaning — even though you dread it — because you want your place to be sparkling when special visitors arrive.

In other situations when free adults feel powerless, e.g. as battered spouses can feel, they are often driven by physical fear of retribution and fear of loss, i.e. powerful dependency needs and wishes. This fear motivates them to stay in a destructive relationship. They may be more afraid of the consequences of leaving the relationship [independence] than they are of the injuries they will suffer if they stay. They fear being alone even if they are physically safe and hidden from the batterer because then, suddenly, they must take care of themselves financially, socially and emotionally, etc. This fear can be stronger than any reality. In contrast, abused children are often powerless because they are not free and so have to both escape and find the same powerful, legal and mental health help and physical safety that is available to adults. This is usually well beyond their emotional and practical ability.

When the motivation for your actions is a sense of obligation or duty (a form of community responsibility), your motivation is indirectly grounded in feelings. In these cases, you are voting with your values. Duty relies on a view of yourself, i.e. a part of your identity that you admire or that would be unthinkable to change. It is often related to a sense of integrity: "I promised I would", "it's my job", or "I owe them this". Check to see if dutiful or doing the right thing was a characteristic you noted in your Diversity Paradigms (see Step I: Self-Awareness – Self-Assessments) and Identity Comparison profiles (see Part II: Self-Development – Identity Comparison). When you see yourself as an honorable or responsible person you would damage your identity if you failed to meet your obligations, e.g. blow off an assignment, disobey orders, or ignore a rather fussy directive of your committee chair about the kind of stamps to put on a social invitation. Acknowledging such changes in identity can be extremely painful.

As we learned in Step I: Self-Awareness under Feeling Management, a Time Out to reflect is the crucial first step for a Considered Response whenever we have an urge or need to act. Then the trick is to distinguish which set of feelings we are responding to and adjust our behavior to take only and all the relevant feelings and circumstances into account first. Then we can consciously choose or design an action that facilitates our reaching both our short and long-term goals, our desired end result and avoid impulsive, destructive actions.

Lack of motivation is a parallel problem. It is also driven by feelings. Unfortunately, it can lead to equally destructive failures to act, like not paying your taxes or rent and not renewing your driver's license. The feelings in these cases are so powerful they override the far more obvious need to act. Rebellion and defiance are often part of them. People who get frozen with fear instead of dashing for safety are endangered by the enormity of their terror which paralyzes their ability to think and act. In less extreme situations, people find themselves unmotivated to do important chores (e.g. balance their budget) or to look for work. In these circumstances, their previous disappointments may not have been processed enough and are bogging them down or perhaps other emotional conflicts like anxiety about failure or fear of success are tangling or tying them in knots [A combination of Feeling Management in Step I: Self-Awareness — starting with naming ALL the feelings — and Decision Making in Step II: Self-Development can help resolve some of these emotional conflicts].

SKILLS

I) REFLECTION TECHNIQUES

Throughout this framework, we have repeatedly recommended taking time out to think things through. Such **time for reflection** is best preserved through **deliberate scheduling**. Take time to **decide** how you plan to **integrate** reflective moments into your life to ensure you allow adequate time in your daily or weekly routine. Vacations every so often are wonderful if you can arrange them, but rarely happen often enough for routine reflection, even though they are very compatible with busy lives. However, a few minutes most days, perhaps early in the morning with a look at your **dreams**, and/or before sleep can be extraordinarily effective. Some people use their commute time. This essential reflective process is also incorporated into **spirituality**, organized **religion**, **meditation, yoga**, and **some martial arts derivatives**, etc. All of these practices support emotional competence development. People also often use music, water from fountains and hot baths, hiking in nature, or a walk in the park.

PRACTICE: JOURNAL REVIEW AND ANALYSIS

Now is the time to consider the actual process of journaling itself. Did you do it? If not, why not? If you did do it, even once, how did you feel about doing it? Was it helpful to write about events and feelings in your journal? As part of the reflection process, take this opportunity to look over your **journal** or notes about what you **planned** to do when you began reading this book. How do they compare to what has actually happened?

When you look back at what you wrote, what did you include? What did you omit? What can you learn about yourself from this review? How can you use this information in your self-development? In what ways can your new insights guide your self-development and empower you in moving forward?

Next, take about ten minutes and make a summary outline of what you think were the main events in your last year related to your personal growth. Arrange them in the same order that they occurred. Always note your feelings about what happened. It is helpful to divide your page into two parallel columns with events on the left side and the corresponding feelings in the right column, opposite each particular action or sentence.

Next, take a look at your **personal growth** itself and the **feelings** you now have about it. List them as they come to mind. The more you practice identifying feelings at all levels, the better your skills will be. Sooner or later, you will likely encounter most of the range of feelings (see Emotional Literacy Tables below) in yourself and/or others — it is often comforting as you reread your journal from time to time to remember that others have felt similarly.

Be sure to **assess your performance** and discuss your self-evaluation (see Step IV: Self-Responsibility — Self-Assessment). Then, **anticipate** the next steps with respect to personal growth. What do you see long-term? As you say **good-bye** to this book, take the **initiative** to compose a satisfying good-bye for yourself that will bring the kind of closure you would like to any **relationships** you may have developed and will change due to you going through this learning and growth process. Also, describe what you have **integrated** from this framework and from other individuals, if anything, and will therefore take with you and use.

Finally, looking towards the future, ask yourself — what do you **anticipate** next year with respect to your personal growth? What do you see beyond that?

II) EXPLORING FEELINGS

a) EMOTIONAL LITERACY OR FEELING FLUENCY

Integrating your feelings fluidly and constructively with your thinking and judgment before you act requires you to know *precisely* which feelings are involved. The term **emotional literacy** is used in most emotional intelligence literature to describe this ability – which includes recognizing, understanding, and expressing feelings. The term **feeling fluency** is an informal term used to refer to talking about feelings in this sophisticated way. Although everyone experiences hundreds of feelings every day and we may recognize many of these emotions, most people are not accustomed to talking about them with ease or specificity. In fact, most people are quite limited in their vocabulary and fluency when describing feelings. This seems to be true whether they are talking about their own feelings, or someone else's.

This difficulty likely comes from limited practice, starting from childhood where feeling fluency may have been neglected or actively discouraged. However, thankfully, emotional literacy/feeling fluency can be learned. The same people that get tongue tied when asked about their feelings can be quite specific and articulate about car engines, hairstyles, computers or food, etc. So, with a similar interest plus exposure to conversations and education about feelings and their essential role in our lives, most people can become fluent and able to use their emotional literacy/feeling fluency skills when they wish.

In one EQD high school workshop, the children were discussing a regrettable event in which a few girls had picked on a fourth girl. Each child in the class was polled about how they felt about the incident. Everyone had feelings, both as a participant or a witness. By the end of the 3rd Feeling Management Step "Name All Your Feelings" (see Step I: Self-Awareness – Feeling Management), there were 45 different feelings written on the board! That "visible" collection of emotions helped the students understand the complex impact of common behaviors and they were able to grasp why such events are so complicated to resolve. Furthermore, they heard contradictory feelings voiced by the same person. The **Emotional Literacy Tables** at the end of this chapter are an emotional competence aid that is especially useful when working alone with your journal.

If you slowly review each of the lists of feelings in the Emotional Literacy Tables you will have an opportunity to explore the myriad of feelings that sweep through you every day, whether they come in light breezes or gale force winds! Ask yourself if you have ever experienced each particular feeling word. Try to recall when and what happened. Then, select one incident you recall from an average day each week, note your feelings, and then check from which columns most of them come. Look for patterns and habits. Notice what evokes the positive feelings and what stirs the negative ones.

If you combine this review with your journaling, you can extend your self-perception of feelings for each one of the 31 columns. The more you practice on daily feelings, the more proficient you will become with your tools before an emotional hurricane hits — if you live in such a zone!

b) FEELING TRANSITIONS

It is often difficult to manage your feelings through sudden changes in your circumstances. This is especially true when your feelings have been very intense, and then you need to "calm down". For example, perhaps you have been very excited about a performance and it is now over, or you are really scared about an exam and you've turned in your paper, or you were thrilled to see someone and now they have gone — then, after such events, you have to switch gears to study, go to sleep or just "get back to normal". What skills do you have for making such transitions in your feelings smoothly?

Think about examples of other people you know, and characters you have seen or read about in the media. How do they typically handle transitions? What is your family pattern with respect to recovering from strong emotions or suddenly being confronted with an emotional situation? Unfortunately, these transitions are often one of the occasions for substance misuse/abuse. What examples of this have you witnessed? How well do they work?

Feeling management can be very effective with feeling transitions. Much of the time will be spent in the 5th Feeling Management Step "Face *All* Your Feelings" (see Step I: Self-Awareness – Feeling Management) if the transition is basically straightforward but involves an enormous range of intensity of feelings.

c) COMMON FEELINGS

The tables at the end of this chapter list many common feelings that people encounter every day. It is included as an aid in naming feelings. Some of them will be emotions that are universally experienced and which are therefore very familiar, such as angry, sad and happy. Others may be less familiar feelings that you only recognize when described. In addition, there may be feelings on the list with which you have no personal experience or which may be totally unknown to you, however, you may encounter them in others so they may become important in your relationships.

A word of caution is important here **about exploring feelings**. Although the Feeling Management process is rarely going to generate many feelings that were not already there because of your life experience, it is important that you **monitor your tolerance** for whatever feelings you encounter. You could occasionally *uncover* more feelings than you want to face at one time. Only explore as far as you feel comfortable identifying and processing because it is occasionally possible to become unwillingly preoccupied with feelings, or even flooded. Select your time to explore your feelings so that it suits the other demands of your life. Remember this Universal Emotional Competence Framework is designed to help you *take charge of your personal growth and development*, this includes pacing yourself, setting realistic goals, and reaching out for help if/when you need it.

If you find yourself more than usually overwhelmed with feelings or nightmares or unable to function as usual, we recommend that you seek some professional help from a psychiatrist or other expert in mental health issues. It is often helpful to start by requesting an evaluation, and using your emotional competence skills and the expert's opinion to decide whom to see and for how long, etc.

PRACTICE: INTEGRATED SKILLS PRACTICE

Set aside an hour to record a current situation in your life for a practice analysis and response on your own. **Use your journal** or a word processor. Follow the outline below and discuss your experience with trusted friends or confidants.

EXAMPLE SITUATION:

Just completing the following process can often clarify an issue for you quite quickly.

1. Make a table with 3 columns, leaving **wide margins**, left and right.
2. **Title** the issue/situation you are dealing with.
3. Note **your goal** for this exercise underneath the title.
4. **Title the left column "Facts"; central column "Feelings" and right column "Emotional Competence (EC) issue".**
5. Write your **factual** account in **chronological order.** Include the nonverbal communications involved too. If you are hand writing, double-space it so that you have room to **add relevant facts** as you think of them later.
6. Note any **speculations/presumptions in *italics/parentheses, e.g. ("I thought she was jealous")*.**
7. Record **feelings in the central column**, opposite the related facts.
8. Read it all over again for **completeness** and **accuracy.** Add missing **facts** and **feelings** as necessary.

PRE-ANALYSIS:

1. **Review** your account to be sure that you have included all the facts you have. Add any missing ones.

2. **Delete/cross out irrelevancies.** Stay focused on the situation and goal you wrote at the beginning underneath the title.

3. Be sure everything is in **chronological** order. Rewrite if necessary.

4. Are the **feelings** throughout written in the central column? Which ones have you omitted? Add them opposite that part of the story and think why you forgot them.

5. Check that speculations/presumptions are all in italics/parentheses. Move them out if necessary.

6. At the end, mention any **dreams** you have had about the topic. Note the incubation question if there was one and the page number in your dream journal where you can look it up if you wish.

ANALYSIS:

1. **Identify the Emotional Competence Concepts, Skills, and Practices** involved in the situation as it occurred. Note them in the right-hand column opposite that part of the story, e.g. Dependency, Motivation impact, Nonverbal Communication, etc.

2. Deal with your **own individual role first**, e.g.:
   a. Do diversity issues fit in anywhere?
   b. Is there a decision to be made?
   c. Which of the major components of self-responsibility apply?
   d. Is this going to affect your philosophy of life or lifestyle?

3. Which **relationship issues** are you dealing with, if any?

4. Assess the **intent/motivations** from your perspective.
   a. Assess your side of the interactions for intent.
   b. Assess the other person's side of the interactions for intent.
   c. Is this a serious disagreement and is negotiation necessary?

5. Assess the **impact** issue from your perspective
   a. Assess the other person's side of the interactions for impact.
   b. Assess your side of the interactions for impact.

6. Apply Feeling Management (see Step I: Self-Awareness — Feeling Management), to as many of the issues as necessary for devising a plan for resolution, e.g.
   a. In "**Face *All* the Feelings**", is loss an issue?
   b. If so, use the **Grief protocol** (see Step II: Self-Development — 6-Stages of Grief) before moving on.

7. To "Choose the Best Result for Now and Later", consider if decision making is an issue. If so, use the A-B-C's of Decisions (See Step II: Self-Development — Decision Making) to make your choice.

8. Lastly, if you had any dreams related to the issue do **descriptive definitions** of 3 major images in your dream, including the setting, which often bridges to the area of life that the dream is addressing. See if you can increase your understanding of the issues. Does your bridge confirm what you have worked out consciously so far? How does it differ? Can you reconcile it in any way?

INTEGRATED SKILLS PRACTICE EXAMPLE

Anecdote [**Facts**]	**Feelings** [narrator]	**EQD Steps for Development**	**Specific Emotional Competence Issues**
Event: I started a new job and was told that my schedule was Monday through Friday from 9a.m. to 5p.m.	I felt **excited** and **happy** about starting my new job.	Self-Development (II):	*Identity Decisions*
After one week at the job I was told by my Supervisor that I needed to attend a 3-day long mandatory training that started at 7 a.m. each day the following week.	I felt **taken aback** and **disappointed**, as this was not something that I had agreed to and I have a lot of responsibilities at home early in the morning – specifically, preparing my children for and taking them to school.	Self-Development (II): Relationships (III): Self – Responsibility (IV):	*Dependency* *Institutional Relationships Conflict Resolution Limit Setting* *Plans and Structure Time management*
Nobody asked for my input.	I felt **unimportant** and **disrespected** that I wasn't asked about this since it varies from what I was originally told about my work schedule.	Self-Awareness (I): Relationship (III):	*Feeling Management* *Conflict Resolution*
I informed my Supervisor of the following points: 1. I do not live in a safe neighborhood and would have to leave my home at 6a.m. — it is still dark at that hour outside — I thus do not feel safe leaving my house so early. 2. I have other responsibilities	I felt **confident** and **self-assured** about voicing my concerns to my supervisor. I also felt **vulnerable** that I would be seen as "not being cooperative".	Self-Awareness (I): Self-Development (II): Relationships (III):	*Feeling management Communication-verbal & nonverbal* *Dependency Decisions* *Motivation vs Impact Other Awareness Conflict Resolution Limit Setting*

		Self-Responsibility (IV):	Initiative
that need attending to during that time – most importantly caring for my children.			
I was told by my Supervisor that I did not have the option to not attending and that the training was mandatory.	I felt **angry, betrayed** and **trapped** because I now felt **pressure** to find a way to make it to the training and had to put my safety at risk.	Relationship (III):	Hierarchical/Power Dynamics Institutional Relationships Conflict Resolution
		Self-Responsibility (IV):	Integrity Power
I then found out that other co-workers were not required to go, and that some who did had more convenient timing options than me.	I felt even more **enraged** and **disrespected**. As now I felt I was being **singled out** and **taken advantage of**.	Self-Awareness (I)	Feeling Management
		Relationships (III)	Conflict Resolution
I decided to make arrangements for child-care in order to go to the training.	I felt **angry** and **conflicted**. I really need the income from this job to take care of myself and my family right now – so I feel **accommodating** and **obligated** to continue to do so. I am also thinking about finding another job as I do not like to be treated this way – but I also do not know if this is a 'one-time thing' – so I feel **cautious** too.	Self-Awareness (I)	Feeling Management
		Self-Development (II)	Dependency Decisions
		Relationship (III)	Motivation vs Impact
		Responsibility (IV)	Initiative Anticipating Problems Money Integrity

PRACTICE: EMOTIONAL LITERACY TABLES

Use the following Emotional Literacy Tables (— a list of common feelings arranged by type) to facilitate clear identification of various emotions when you discuss your feelings with others and/or document in your journal, etc. As you review the tables, distinguish between 1) familiar feelings, 2) feelings you have experienced before, 3) feelings that you recognize — but have never experienced, and 4) feelings that are unknown to you. Doing so will increase your feeling fluency. By increasing your feeling fluency, you will not only become more proficient at discussing events and appropriately including your major feelings, but you will also refine your ability to make subtle differentiations between feelings in yourself and others.

Pleasurable Feelings

Happiness	Amusement	Quiet Pleasure	Interest
blissful	clownish	amiable	awed
brilliant	bubbly	calm	concentrating
charming	giddy	comforted	contemplative
cheerful	gleeful	competent	curious
cheery	idiotic	contented	eager
chipper	jolly	easy	engaged
creative	jovial	glad	enthralled
delighted	merry	happy	fascinated
ecstatic	mirthful	mellow	focused
elated	mischievous	peaceful	interested
enchanted	playful	pleasant	intrigued
enthusiastic	silly	pleased	meditative
exalted	tickled	relaxed	mesmerized
excited	whimsical	relieved	observant
exhilarated	zany	satisfied	reflective
exuberant		serene	spellbound
gay (old usage)		soothed	thoughtful
good		touched	watchful
great		warm	
happy			
high			
joyful			
joyous			
jubilant			

marvelous			
optimistic			
splendid			
successful			
thrilled			
triumphant			
turned on			
wonderful			

Positive and Mixed Feelings

Confidence	Self-assurance	Surprise	Caution & Concern
adamant	capable	alarm	alert
aggressive	confident	astonished	careful
ambitious	convinced	astounded	caring
arrogant	masterful	awed	cautious
assertive	mastery	awestruck	commiseration
assured	proud	consternation	compassionate
boastful	satisfied	boggled	concerned
calm	self confident	disbelieving	empathy
certain	successful	flabbergasted	expectant
compelled		freaked out	goodwill
competitive		incredulous	pity
confident		shocked	protective
courageous		startled	prudent
daring		surprised	reflective
determined		taken aback	sympathetic
effective		stunned	tenderness
encouraged			thoughtful
enthusiastic			touched
fearless			worry, worried
firm			
formidable			
hardy			
inspired			
on			
potent			
powerful			
resolved			
self-assured			
strong			
successful			
sure			
vain			
zealous			

Painful Feelings

General Distress	Anxiety	Grief & Sadness	Anger
abject	agitated	anguished	abrasive
bad	agonized	apathetic	aggravated
brittle	alarmed	bereaved	aggressive
burdened	churned up	bereft	aggrieved
confounded	defensive	blue	angry, mad
consternation	frantic	chagrined	annoyed
crushed	freaked	deflated	bitter
discontented	frenzied	dejected	blaming
discordant	fretted	depressed	combative
disgruntled	garrulous	desolate	crabby
displeased	high strung	despairing	curmudgeonly
dissatisfied	hysterical	despondent	destructive
dissonant	impatient	disappointed	disgruntled
disturbed	nervous	disconsolate	edgy
doomed	obsessive	discouraged	enraged
drained	panicked	dismal	evil
envious	rattled	down, downhearted	exasperated
evil	restless	downcast	frustrated
exhausted	tempestuous	forlorn	fired up, fuming
a failure	tumultuous	gloomy	furious, fury
fragile	turbulent	glum	grumpy, prickly
hurt	revved up	heartbroken	hate, hate filled
invisible	self conscious	lonely	heated up
jealous	unsettled	lost	hostile
let down	worried	low	hot under the collar
miserable		maudlin	irritable, irritated
negative		melancholy	jealous
oppressed		mournful	mean, spiteful
overwhelmed		nostalgic	pouting
pain		numb, numbness	punitive
pained		pain, pained	rankled
perturbed		pining	reproachful
unhappy		resigned	resentful
unwell		sad	riled, irate
upset		sorrow	surly
worthless		suicidal	vengeful
		tearful	venomous
		unhappy	vicious

Painful and Negative Feelings

Fear	Shame & Guilt	Disapproval	Worthlessness
afraid	abashed	abhorrence	abject, bad
alarmed	apologetic	ashamed	cheap
anxious	ashamed	aversion	cheesy
apprehensive	chagrined	contemptuous	despicable
cautious	contrite	despicable	devalued
cowardly	degraded	disdained	dirty
defensive	despicable	disgusted	dispensable
dread, dreading	embarrassed	distaste	disposable
fear, fearful	exposed	judgmental	dumb
fright, frightened	guilty	loathing	evil
horrified	humiliated	nauseated	horrible
insecure	miserable	repelled	inadequate
intimidated	mortified	repulsed	incompetent
leery	regretful	revolted	inept
nervous	remorseful	scorn	insignificant
panic, panicky	responsible	sickened	irrelevant
paranoid	sheepish		low self esteem
scared	squirming		no good
suspicious			pariah
terrified			pointless
terror			replaceable
terror-stricken			silly
uncertain			stupid
unsafe			ugly
vigilant			unappreciated
vulnerable			unessential
wary			unimportant
worried			unlovable
			useless
			valueless
			worthless
			wretched

Negative Feelings

Immobilization	Shock	Confusion	Disinterest
ambivalent	aghast	baffled	bored
avoidant	appalled	befuddled	careless
conflicted	astounded	bemused	disaffected
demoralized	battered	bewildered	disengaged
entrenched	blown away	cockeyed	indifferent
immobilized	disbelieving	crazy	oblivious
impotent	disillusioned	discombobulated	off
indecisive	dumbfounded	disoriented	uncaring
ineffective	horrified	mind boggled	uninterested
ineffectual	overwhelmed	muddled	unmoved
lazy	shaken	mystified	unobservant
mired	shattered	nonplussed	
obstinate	speechless	perplexed	
paralyzed	staggered	puzzled	
powerless	startled	unclear	
pulled	stunned		
pushed	stupefied		
resistant	thunderstruck		
rigid			
rushed			
stubborn			
stuck			
torn			
trapped			
undecided			
unmotivated			

Positive & Power Related Interpersonal Feelings

(Positive feelings usually enhance relationships)

Positive Attachment	Sexual attraction	Cooperation	Power
affectionate	ambivalent	accommodating	coercive
appreciative	amorous	collaborative	collaborative
approving	anxious	compliant	comfortable
attached	attracted	compromising	compliant
attracted	awkward	conciliatory	cooperative
blissful	bewitched	eager	critical
caring	cautious	flexible	dominant
connected	conflicted	helpful	ecstatic
cuddly	desire	obedient	entitled
dependent	exposed	obligated	excited
devotion	flirtatious	persuasive	exposed
doting	impulsive	pleasing	fearful, terrified
fondness	infatuated	responsible	good, happy
friendly	innocent	satisfied	hierarchical
grateful	interested	tenacious	inadequate
liking	intrigued	trusting	malicious
lovesick	lascivious		manipulative
loving	lusty, lustful		masterful
protective	modest		passive aggressive
respect	passionate		powerful
responsive	playful		powerless
tender	prudish		proud
vulnerable	safe		rebellious
warmth	sated		reluctant
	sensual		resentful
	sexy		resistant
	shy		responsible
	threatened		sadistic
	unsafe		servile
	urgent		solicitous
			spiteful
			submissive
			subversive
			tense, nervous
			uncomfortable
			unhappy
			vengeful
			worried, anxious

Negative Interpersonal Feelings

(Often signaling difficulty in relationships)

Trepidation	Distance	Negative Attachment	Abrasiveness
apprehensive	betrayed	battered	arrogant
bashful	cold	bullied	coercive
cautious	cut off	cheated	conceited
exposed	disapproving	competitive	confrontational
inferior	disconnected	desire to bully	contrary
insecure	estranged	disrespected	defiant
overwhelmed	indifferent	dominated	dismissive
reluctant	isolated	dominating	disobedient
self-conscious	judged	envious	erratic
shy	outside	exposed	insubordinate
threatened	rebuffed	injured	oblivious
timid	rejected	insulted	oppositional
vulnerable	repelled	jaded	overconfident
	uncaring	jealous	provocative
	undesirable	offended	rebellious
	unwanted	put upon	resistant
	withdrawn	retaliatory	self-absorbed
		victimized	self-centered
		vulnerable	self-deceptive
			selfish
			self-satisfied
			stubborn
			superior
			unaware
			unpredictable
			unreasonable
			vain

No feelings/unable to identify feelings (alexithymia)

Unrecognized	Detached	Somaticized
beyond feelings	cold	blushing
deadened	disinterested	fist clenching
dazed	indifferent	headache
denial	neutral	heart pounding
disconnected	uninvolved	leg bouncing
empty	unmoved	muscle tension
in shock	"whatever"	shaking
"no big deal"		stomach upset
nothing		teeth grinding
numb		trembling
out of touch		
shut down		
spaced, spaced out		
unaware		

SUMMARY

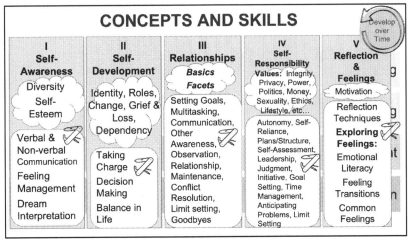

Fig 5. 1 Addition of Step V: Reflection & Feelings Concepts and Skills

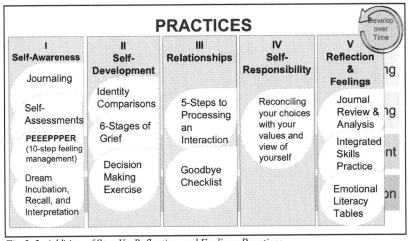

Fig 5. 2 Addition of Step V: Reflection and Feelings Practices.

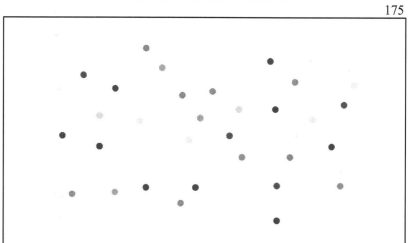

NOTES & CONTACTS

NOTES & CONTACTS

NOTES & CONTACTS

Made in the USA
San Bernardino, CA
04 August 2019